The President's Law Firm

Studies in Law and Politics

David A. Schultz
General Editor

Vol. 7

The Studies in Law and Politics series
is part of the Peter Lang Politics and Economics list.
Every volume is peer reviewed and meets
the highest quality standards for content and production.

PETER LANG
New York • Bern • Berlin
Brussels • Vienna • Oxford • Warsaw

Billy W. Monroe

The President's Law Firm

The Office of Legal Counsel from Roosevelt to Trump

PETER LANG
New York • Bern • Berlin
Brussels • Vienna • Oxford • Warsaw

Library of Congress Cataloging-in-Publication Data

Names: Monroe, Billy W., author.
Title: The president's law firm: the office of legal counsel from Roosevelt to Trump / Billy W. Monroe.
Description: New York: Peter Lang, 2021.
Series: Studies in law and politics; vol. 7 | ISSN 1083-3366
Includes bibliographical references.
Identifiers: LCCN 2020052458 (print) | LCCN 2020052459 (ebook)
ISBN 978-1-4331-8488-8 (hardback) | ISBN 978-1-4331-8489-5 (ebook pdf)
ISBN 978-1-4331-8490-1 (epub) | ISBN 978-1-4331-8491-8 (mobi)
Subjects: LCSH: United States. Department of Justice. Office of Legal Counsel—History. | Presidents—United States. | Government attorneys—United States.
Classification: LCC KF5107 .M66 2021 (print) | LCC KF5107 (ebook) | DDC 342.73/062—dc23
LC record available at https://lccn.loc.gov/2020052458
LC ebook record available at https://lccn.loc.gov/2020052459
DOI 10.3726/b18011

Bibliographic information published by **Die Deutsche Nationalbibliothek**. **Die Deutsche Nationalbibliothek** lists this publication in the "Deutsche Nationalbibliografie"; detailed bibliographic data are available on the Internet at http://dnb.d-nb.de/.

80 Broad Street, 5th floor, New York, NY 10004
www.peterlang.com

Contents

Preface

The subject of this book is the Office of Legal Counsel (OLC) in the U.S. Department of Justice (USDOJ). This book is intended to be a comprehensive study of the Office, including its history, functions, and impact on governmental decisions. While the impact of the OLC is mainly on the office of the President, and on the legal positions of the executive branch, the OLC's actions also influence legislative decisions of Congress and judicial decisions in court cases. Overtime, the OLC has extensively evolved. Today, the office straddles the line between politics and law, as well as interacting with the rest of the Department of Justice. The Office of Legal Counsel provides an essential role for both the President and the rest of the national government, but it does not receive nearly the attention or scrutiny it deserves. This book is intended to illuminate the inner workings of the OLC, its importance to other branches to the government, and the impact that the OLC makes behind the scenes on the lives of everyday Americans. The title of the book is a reference to the nickname often given to the OLC. Although the Office had various names over the years, for clarity, the name Office of the Legal Counsel, or OLC, is used throughout the book.

The central audience of this book is likely to be legal practitioners and scholars. Lawyers, judges, and law professors will likely find this book helpful, but scholars of law and politics will hopefully find this book to be an excellent supplement to more traditional sources of information. Upper-level undergraduates, graduate students, historians, and professors of American politics will find this book useful, but it may be in terms of constitutional law, legal history, and public law that this book provides the strongest contribution. While the book is written in such a fashion that general readers and other interested observers of the American legal system can understand it, the material itself is somewhat dense and technical. This book is mainly a scholarly text, but it will be valuable outside of the classroom for supplemental reading in courses that specialize in judicial politics, process, or the legal profession at either undergraduate, graduate, or law school levels.

The author of this book is a tenured political science professor specializing in American politics, public law, and legal history. The Office of Legal Counsel has long been a fascination of the author. It was a particular interest as a graduate student during the George W. Bush administration. The use of executive orders has become a focal point for both scholars and the public in recent years. It seems clear that many people, whether in the legal field or simply interested in the state of politics today, wish to understand the significance of the Office of Legal Counsel, and why the OLC seems to be involved in so many of the ongoing situations that are discussed by the media. The desire to learn more about the OLC, combined with a lack of success in finding quality sources of information, provided plenty of inspiration for the author to write this book.

Chapter One

Introduction

By delegation from the Attorney General (AG), the Assistant Attorney General (AAG) in charge of the Office of Legal Counsel (OLC) provides reliable legal advice to the President and all the Executive Branch agencies. The Office drafts legal opinions of the Attorney General and also provides its own written opinions and oral advice in response to requests from the Counsel to the President, the various agencies of the Executive Branch, and offices within the Department. Such requests typically deal with legal issues of particular complexity and importance where two or more agencies are in disagreement. The Office also is responsible for advising on issues of constitutionality, reviewing pending legislation, and providing the Executive branch with legal advice.

When the President proposes to issue an executive order or proclamation, he cannot do so unilaterally despite the way that it may have been presented in the popular media. When a presidential candidate announces, for example, that their first act if elected will be to issue an executive order on a particular matter, the newly elected President cannot do so without the approval of the OLC. It is the OLC's responsibility to ensure that executive orders and proclamations proposed to be issued by the President are reviewed by the Office of Legal Counsel for form and legality, as are various other matters that require the President's formal approval.

Professor Arthur Garrison (2012, 2013), whose works were cited throughout this book, was kind enough to allow an interview on May 27, 2020. He emphasized that the Office of Legal Counsel is given the job of protecting the Office of the President as an *institution*. The OLC must also follow the rule of law and are intended to be as impartial as possible. The opinions of the OLC are considered to be definitive for everyone in the executive branch except for the office of the Solicitor General. The problem, of course, is that the opposite view, which is that the OLC must be loyal to the President's policy objectives. In several recent presidencies this dichotomy has caused a huge dilemma and has resulted in a great deal of outcry, particularly because of incidents in the Bush administration (Garrison, 2020). This clash is discussed further in Chapter 9, in conjunction with a discussion of John Yoo's 2001 memos, which supported President Bush's view that he had the right to handle suspected terrorists as he wished.

Cover (2012) argues that the production of OLC memos is a collective action. He suggests that the current system fails to hold supervisory attorneys accountable for the contents of the opinions, and thus weakens the opportunity for an attorney to dissent with the presidential viewpoint. By holding the supervisory attorneys responsible for the legal opinions reflected in the OLC memos, there would be more accountability and thus more forethought before the memos were issued. The opinions would more nearly reflect a balanced perspective of the legal points, rather than merely reflecting the presidential view (Cover, 2012). Cover argues that the time has come to mandate a revision of the professional rules of conduct for those who oversee the OLC, in order to ensure that the advice given to the President reflects the law and not the President's preferences.

From the beginning of the Carter Administration through the first year of Obama's administration, OLC produced 245 opinions that were available to the public. Of these 245 opinions, 193 (or 79%) fully supported the President's position. An additional twenty positions, or 8%, supported some portion of the President's position. Thirty-two opinions, or 13%, were in opposition to the President's stated viewpoint (Cover, 2012, 276; Morrison 2010 supra note 13, at 1476–79). However, as Cover pointed out, and other analysts have argued, it is very difficult to discover the true number of OLC memoranda for any time period, because the memorandum can be either classified or withheld from the public. Thus, the number of memos in support of the President's opinion can be higher, or lower.[1] Cover (2012) argues that the number of memorandum in opposition to the President are probably undercounted, simply because they have been withheld from the public and are thus unlikely to reflect the President's opinion (276, note 36). Regardless of what the eventual outcome is, it is clear immediately that there must be some procedure implemented for numbering *and accounting for* executive orders and their content. Even if the order is classified, the subject of the order should not be, and the subject of the order(s) should not be withheld from the public in order to remain transparent.

It is important to understand that in addition to serving as, in effect, outside counsel for the other agencies of the Executive Branch, the Office of Legal Counsel also plays a special role within the Department itself. The OLC reviews orders that have been proposed by the Attorney General and also all regulations that need the AG's approval before being released. It also performs any special assignments that might be referred by the Attorney General or the Deputy Attorney General (2017). Although executive orders existed prior to 1933, they were not numbered until Franklin D. Roosevelt's stay in office. It would be difficult to determine how many orders actually existed, with any assuredness, until the orders began to be numbered.[2] Table 1 reflects the issuance of orders from the beginning of Franklin D. Roosevelt's presidency to the Trump presidency in September, 2019. It should be noted that the "years in office" is based on information taken directly from the Archives and may not reflect complete years. Thus, the "terms" column provides more detail.

The information in Table 1 was gathered from several sources inside the Federal Register of the National Archives. As of this writing, President Donald Trump's information has not been added to the Executive Orders Disposition Tables Index ("Executive orders disposition tables index," 2019), which provides data on executive orders

Table 1. Executive Orders

#	President/ Political Party	Total Orders	App. Yrs in Office	Presidential Service Dates	Terms
32	Franklin D. Roosevelt (D)	3728	12	1933–1945	3 full terms plus 2 mos. and 23 days (4422 days)
33	Harry S. Truman (D)	896	8	1945–1953	3 yrs, 9 mos and 8 days followed by a full term (2840 days)
34	Dwight D. Eisenhower (R)	486	8	1953–1961	2 full terms (2922 days)
35	John F. Kennedy (D)	214	2	1961–1963	2 yrs, 2 mos, 2 days (1036 days)
36	Lyndon B. Johnson (D)	324	5	1963–1969	1 yr, 1 month, 29 days followed by a full term (1886 days)
37	Richard Nixon (R)	346	5	1969–1974	1 full term followed by 1 yr, 6 mos, 20 days (2027 days)
38	Gerald R. Ford (R)	169	2	1974–1977	2 yrs, 5 mos, 11 days (895 days)
39	Jimmy Carter (D)	320	4	1977–1981	1 full term (1461 days)
40	Ronald Reagan (R)	381	8	1981–1989	2 full terms (2922 days)
41	George Bush (R)	166	4	1989–1993	1 full term (1461 days)
42	William J. Clinton - D	364	8	1993–2001	2 full terms (2922 days)
43	George W. Bush - R	291	8	2001–2009	2 full terms (2922 days)
44	Barack Obama - D	276	8	2009–2017	2 full terms (2922 days)
45	Donald Trump - R	122	3	2017–present	2017-present

from Franklin D. Roosevelt through Barack Obama. President Trump's executive orders are stored in a separate area of the Federal Register ("Executive orders," 2019). Throughout the course of this book, information on executive orders from the Archives and the Federal Register will be examined in relation to actions from the Office of Legal Counsel.

As significant as the description of the OLC implies it is – especially in the current political climate where recent Presidents (especially President Trump) see executive orders as their most effective governing tool – the reality is that the OLC is one of the most understudied agencies in the national government in terms of books or scholarly journal articles in peer reviewed journals in political science or related disciplines. Even judicial process textbooks spend much more time explaining the role of the Attorney General, Solicitor General, or U.S. Attorneys than they do for the OLC. In fact, David Klaidman, in an article written for Newsweek, has referred to the OLC as:

> The most important government office you've never heard of. Among its bosses -- before they went on the Supreme Court -- were William Rehnquist and Antonin Scalia. Within the executive branch, including the Pentagon and Central Intelligence Agency, the OLC acts as a kind of mini Supreme Court. Its carefully worded opinions are regarded as binding precedent -- final say on what the president and all his agencies can and cannot legally do. (Klaidman, 2006, para. 11).

Still, there are books that contain information about the OLC. Generally, however, the OLC is not discussed as a central topic in books or journal articles. The books or articles that do discuss the OLC cover the Office as a secondary topic by focusing on opinions produced by the OLC that are worthy of scrutiny. The most famous example are books written in the early 2000s that focus on the so-called "terror memos" written by John Yoo to defend the Bush Administration's position or decisions made regarding torture, waterboarding, and other interrogation techniques used to gain intelligence in fighting the War on Terror (Yoo, 2007, 2008). Yoo's books come from a position of experience: he was a deputy assistant attorney general in the OLC from 2001 to 2003 and had been general counsel of the U.S. Senate Judiciary Committee from 1995–1996. He also has served as clerk for Justice Clarence Thomas of the U.S. Supreme Court. Jack Goldsmith, who became head of legal counsel immediately following John Yoo, was more conservative in nature and action. His books provide a counterpoint to Yoo's opinion; they both deserve a place on the serious Constitutionalist's bookshelf.

Goldsmith's book entitled *The Terror Presidency: Law and Judgement Inside the Bush Administration* (2007) is an excellent example of a more conservative interpretation of the law, leading to Goldsmith's opinion that previous OLC staff (including Yoo) had gone astray. Lavitt (2010) supported that contention; he suggests that Yoo conducted criminal actions in his position in the OLC during the Bush administration.

Goldsmith's 2012 book entitled *Power and Constraint: The Accountable Presidency After 9/11 (2012)* moderated some of his previous opinions, however, and suggested that as the president's powers have expanded, so have the constraints, and thus accountability, placed upon him. This book, the one in the reader's hand, examines presidential histories as they intertwine with the OLC, providing a unique perspective on both the organization and the Presidential and legal positions of the executive branch that stem from the OLC's decisions.

In recent times, the OLC has received attention when the question was raised whether the agency approved executive orders written by President Trump regarding the travel ban into specified Muslim nations. Trump's presidency has been very controversial, and the travel ban question remains under litigation. It is thus a reasonable assumption that analysts in the future will produce additional books that investigate the activities of the OLC. The book you hold in your hands is somewhat unique; it is being written in the days closely following the Supreme Court's ruling that President Trump could dramatically limit asylum seekers while the larger issue of travel bans is being litigated. The ruling means that the United States will not accept asylum applications from individuals (including unaccompanied children) unless they have first applied to their country of transit and are rejected (Liptak, 2019). The case will undoubtedly return to the Supreme Court, so it is very important for scholars and citizens alike to understand the legal implications of this decision before the Court rules again. A partial list of existing works that discuss the OLC can be found at the end of this book, for the reader's ease in continuing to research this topic.

There are also law review articles related to the OLC; several of them are essentially seminal. Dawn Johnsen, a former Acting Assistant Attorney General, published guidelines in the *Indiana Law Journal* describing how lawyers in the OLC should perform their duties (Johnsen, 2006). Stare Decisis in the Office of Legal Counsel studied the importance of precedents for the OLC and was published in the *Columbia Law Review* (Morrison, 2010). Trevor Morrison, the author of that article, also served as an attorney with the OLC. Arthur Garrison (2013) published an article in the *Albany Law Review* that studied the reasons that opinions by the Attorney General and the Office of Legal Counsel are significant (Garrison, 2013). These articles, and other similar ones, provide a valuable source of information for this project, and will be explored at length in subsequent chapters. The Garrison article explicitly summarizes the existing research on the OLC. The studies cited are relatively recent, are centered around very few topics (mainly the War on Terror memos) and are mostly written by former employees of the OLC.

Although a handful of books and articles have been mentioned that provide insight into the OLC, the importance of the organization is completely disproportionate to the existing research. This relative lack of attention is probably the most important reason why another book about the OLC, and particularly the OLC's input into Presidential decision-making vis a vis proclamations and Executive Orders is significant. In its own way, this book is unique, and depending on the reader's specific interests in the legal and presidential fields might be considered exciting.

Organizational Structure of the Justice Department and the OLC

The Justice Department has a complex organization and an equally complex organizational structure. At the time of this writing, the most recent organization chart, denoting the DOJ's structure, had been approved by Jeff Sessions in 2018. The chart in Figure 1 is reproduced from the Organization Manual of the DOJ ("Organization, mission and functions manual," 2012, Organizational Chart).

General Organization

The U.S. Department of Justice is overseen by the U.S. Attorney General and the Deputy Attorney General. The next level of management is comprised of the Solicitor General, and the Associate Attorney General (AAG). The Solicitor General oversees the Office of the Solicitor General. The Office of Legislative Affairs, the Office of Legal Policy, the Office of Tribal Justice, the Office of Public Affairs, and the Office of Legal Counsel are under the direct line of oversight from the Deputy Attorney General and the Attorney General.

The Associate Attorney General is responsible for a dozen organizations within the DOJ. Office of Justice Programs, Community Oriented Policing Services (COPS), the Executive Office for U.S. Trustees, the Office of Information Policy, the Office on Violence Against Women, and the Foreign Claims Settlement Commission are under the control of the Associate Attorney General. The Civil Rights Division, Antitrust Division, Tax Division, Civil Division, Environment & Natural Resources Division, and Community Relations Service are also under the supervision of the Associate Attorney General.

The Deputy Attorney General is responsible for a tremendous number of additional programs, including the Federal Bureau of Investigation (FBI), the Criminal Division, the Drug Enforcement Administration (DEA), the Bureau of Prisons, the Executive Office for U.S. Attorneys, the U.S. Marshals Service, the U.S. Attorneys,

INTERPOL Washington, and the Bureau of Alcohol, Tobacco, Firearms, & Explosives (BATFE). The final branches of the organization are also overseen by the Deputy Attorney General. This final branch contains the National Security Division, the Office of Professional Responsibility, the Office of the Inspector General, the Office of the Pardon Attorney, the Justice Management Division, the U.S. Parole Commission, the Executive Office for Immigration Review, the Executive Office for Organized Crime Drug Enforcement Task Forces, and the Professional Responsibility Advisory Office.

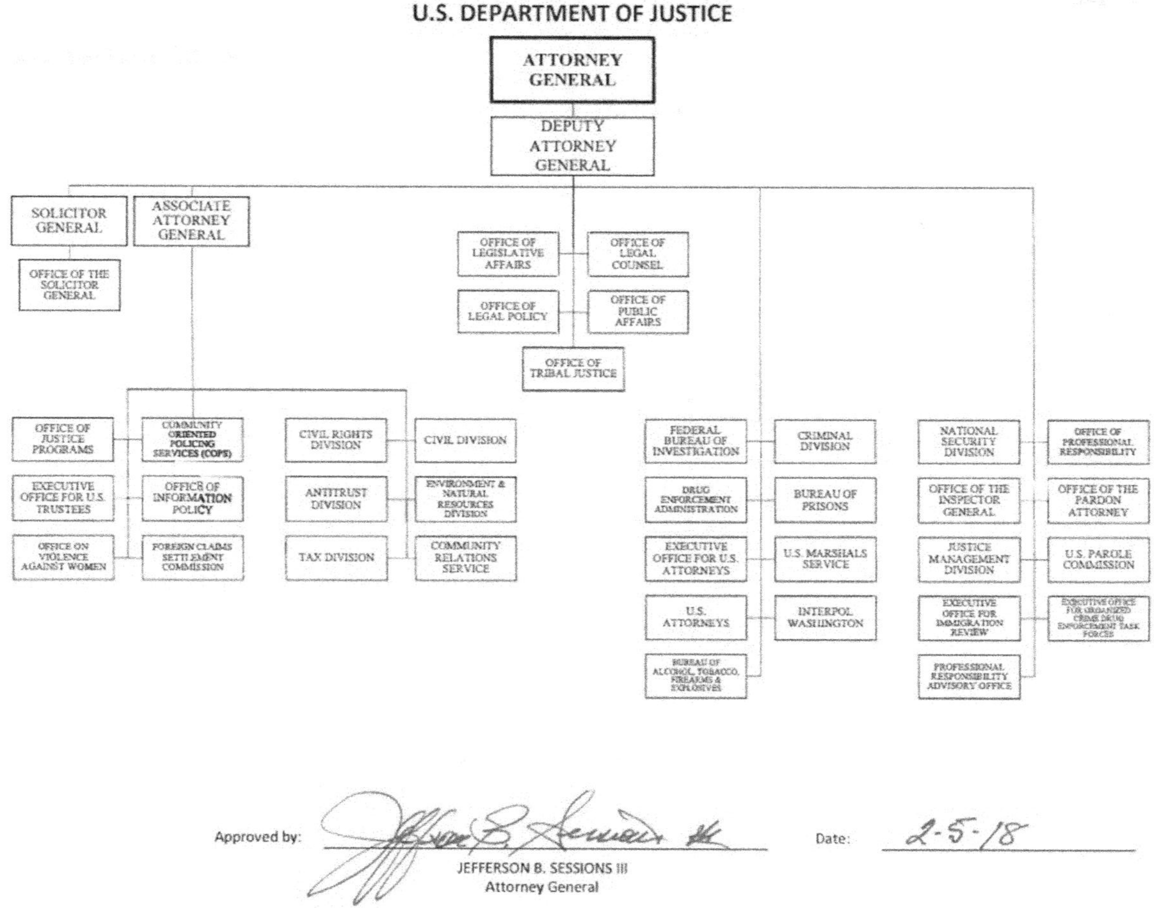

Figure 1. Department of Justice Organization Chart

Justice Management Division

The Justice Management Division of the Department of Justice is comprised of the Attorney General, the Deputy Attorney General, and the Associate Attorney General. The Attorney General is one of the oldest offices in the United States; it was created in 1789 by the Judiciary Act, over 80 years before the Department of Justice was established. The Attorney General was established as the head of the Department of Justice; the AG is responsible for all of the U.S. Attorneys and any counsel in a legal action which represents the United States ("Organization, mission & functions manual: Attorney General, Deputy and Associate," 2014).

Office of the Attorney General. The AG's job description is varied. The AG not only represents the U.S. Attorneys and counsel representing the U.S. in legal matters, but also supervises the operation and administration of all of the offices, boards, divisions, and bureaus in the Department. Whenever an opinion of law is required on legal matters for the President, the Cabinet, or the Executive branch, the AG ensures the opinion is provided. When positions are open for appointment in the federal judiciary or the U.S. Attorneys, or the U.S. Marshals, the AG makes recommendations to the President on those appointments. The AG can represent the interests of the U.S. in front of the Supreme Court; he or she can also choose to simply supervise that representation. At the same time, if the U.S. has interests in other courts, or is a party in those other courts, then the AG has a responsibility to ensure those interests are represented. Finally, they are required to either carry out or supervise duties that are defined in Executive Orders or are required by existing (or future) statutes ("Organization, mission & functions manual: Attorney General, Deputy and Associate," 2014).

Many of the past Attorneys General will be familiar with Americans. Their names have been "in the news" so often that some of them have become household names. Robert F. Kennedy (1961–1964), Ramsey Clark (1966–1969), Janet Reno (1993–2001), Eric H. Holder, Jr. (2001 and 2009–2015), John Ashcroft (2001–2005), Loretta Lynch (2015–2017), Jeff Sessions (2017–2018) and William Barr (1991–1993 and 2019–2021) (Forrester, 2013) are AGs that have become household names because of the decisions that they were responsible for making. These AGs, as well as other lesser-known Attorney Generals, will be discussed in the appropriate chapters of this book, along with other members of the OLC who may have distinguished themselves or contributed notable information.

Office of the Deputy Attorney General. The Office of the Deputy Attorney General (ODAG) was created in 1950 by Attorney General J. Howard McGrath. The ODAG is appointed by the President and confirmed by the Senate. The ODAG supervises 25 components in the DOJ and has 93 U.S. Attorneys reporting to him or her. In addition, the Associate Attorney General supervises 13 components; the ODAG is indirectly responsible for them as well. The overall mission of the ODAG is to assist the AG in the development and supervision of programs and policies.

The Deputy Attorney General (DAG) has all the power of the AG, and all of the authority, unless a particular power has been reserved specifically for the AG. The DAG represents the Justice Department at meetings to coordinate the Homeland Security Council and the National Security Council. Part of the DAG's responsibility is to maintain enough staff that DOJ's policies can be addressed.

A number of legal activities are reserved to the DAG. The DAG authorizes searches and electronic surveillance, makes recommendations as to whether or not questioned cases should seek the death penalty, and recommends whether or not the President should pardon or commute sentences of individuals. The DAG also interfaces with the White House on any timely and pending criminal issues. If acts of terrorism occur, or civil disturbances, the DAG is appointed to control what the DOJ's reaction is. The DAG establishes what the national priorities on crime will be, after consulting with the AG. The DAG also manages programs that are considered high priority in the Office of the Deputy Attorney General. Finally, like millions of employed Americans, the final line of the DAG's job description is to accomplish other duties as assigned ("Organization, mission & functions manual: Attorney General, Deputy and Associate," 2014).

Office of the Associate Attorney General. The Office of the Associate Attorney General (OASG) was created in 1977 by an Attorney General Order. The Associate Attorney General (ASG) is the third highest official at the DOJ, making the ASG a primary member of the AG's senior management. The ASG advises the AG and DAG relating to policies and programs. The ASG will:

> Supervise the work of the Civil, Civil Rights, Antitrust, Tax, and Environment and Natural Resources Divisions. The ASG also has oversight responsibility for the Office of Justice Programs, the Office of Community Oriented Policing Services, the Access to Justice Initiative, the Office of Dispute Resolution, the Office of Information Policy, the Community Relations Service, the Executive Office for United States Trustees, Office on Violence Against Women and the Foreign Claims Settlement Commission. The ASG also shares with the DAG oversight responsibility for the Office of Tribal Justice. ("Organization, mission & functions manual: Attorney General, Deputy and Associate," 2014, final para.)

Functions of the OLC

The Office of Legal Counsel was developed to focus on constitutional questions/issues, executive orders, and defending the Presidential Administration in court. These functions of the AG's office are established under 28 U.S.C. 511–513. This code allows the AG to provide opinions or advice on questions related to law when the President requires him or her to do so, or when the executive head of departments or military departments request ("Organization, mission and functions manual: Office of Legal Counsel," 2012). Any component of the DOJ that wishes legal advice or assistance is entitled to have it; all they need to do is ask the OLC for that assistance.

The OLC is responsible for drafting formal opinions to be issued by the AG. It is also able to give its own opinions to the executive heads of departments and agencies, and to issue opinions to the White House. The OLC reviews all of the executive orders that the President intends to release, for form and legality. The OLC also reviews intended Presidential proclamations, as well as regulations that need to be approved either by the President or by the AG. In addition, when legal questions arise as a result of operations within the DOJ or the administration of the DOJ, the OLC is empowered to issue opinions to both the AG and the heads of departments. The OLC is also the department that advises the AG on issues relating to the Board of Immigration Appeals. Finally, the OLC studies proposed legislation that has been sent to the DOJ for comments. The OLC also reports to the Office of Management and Budget regarding bills that are under consideration ("Organization, mission and functions manual: Office of Legal Counsel," 2019).

Origins of the OLC and Evolution of the Justice Department

Steven A. Engel is currently the Assistant Attorney General in charge of the OLC. Earlier in this chapter, it was reported that the AG's position was established in 1789 by the Judiciary Act. It was not until 1870 that the DOJ was created, so that the AG would have support as they carried out their duties. The AG is a member of the Cabinet that advises the active President. From the beginning of our nation, it was clear that the actions the President took would need to be in compliance with the law. While the American system is built on a program of checks and balances, and congressional oversight would provide some level of protection against Presidential misdeeds, it was not enough. Even limited judicial review of Presidential actions, after the fact, was not enough. Presidents themselves were responsible for compliance with the law. They needed to comply not only with any statutory laws or local legal requirements, but also with the requirements of the Constitution.

As presidents are being sworn in, they take a pledge to "preserve, protect, and defend the Constitution" (U.S. CONST. art. II, § 1, cl. 8.). If the President is to effectively execute the laws of the land, they must first know what the laws are. As Johnsen (2006, 1345) pointed out, in order to obey the Constitutional directives regarding their obligations to the law, the Presidents also need good legal advice.

George Washington, the first President, needed to have legal questions answered. He concluded that the Supreme Court would be the logical organization to provide him with the information he needed. For their part, however, the Court sent Washington back to the officers of the executive branch to seek his answers. This marked the beginning of the dependence on the Attorney General, which continued until the

Office of Legal Counsel was instituted. Today, the OLC has the final say on interpretation of most legal issues, although the AG or the President can override them under some circumstances. Johnsen (2004) provides a discussion of these circumstances.

The OLC has typically worked in relative obscurity, up until the time of the Bush administration, when word of Abu Ghraib was leaked to the world. When the memo, entitled *Standards of Conduct for Interrogation* was released, it appeared to many readers to be a primer for how to conduct torture on our enemies. The net result was that President Bush signed into law prohibitions on many kinds of torture, and *Guidelines for the President's Legal Advisors (including "Principles to Guide the Office of Legal Counsel ")* (Johnsen, 2006) were released. The OLC guidelines will be discussed in later chapters as appropriate.

Thesis of the Book

The goal, or thesis, of this book is to provide a comprehensive study of the Office of Legal Counsel and how the role has evolved over time. Special attention is given to changes that have occurred from one presidential administration to another. These changes are particularly important to American history and to the current American governmental structure because the OLC impacts the office of the President and the operation of the executive branch to such a great extent.

Research Methodology Utilized in the Book

Given that it has already been stated that material on the topic of the OLC is difficult to find, the question naturally arises as to where the information for this book came from, and how the research for the book was conducted. While the strictest standard would have been to conduct archival research utilizing only government documents and OLC opinions, the field has so much more to offer. It is not enough to ask what happened, which could be determined by perusing the documents and the opinions. Instead, legal scholars in particular want to know *why* things happened, and *how*, and how these actions may impact future opinions and executive operations.

The case of impeachment of President Trump is a good example. It is not enough to look at current OLC opinions on the topic of impeachment or on the possibility of charging the current president with a crime. Rather, to get a good perception of what can, and cannot occur at any point, additional information needed to be acquired. This book is mostly qualitative in nature and utilizes historical document analysis, case studies and interviews (when possible). In addition, news articles and commentaries from credible media sources are utilized when appropriate, along with scholarly works and books.

Gray (or grey) literature, or literature that is significant but that is not necessarily listed in academic databases, can also contribute meaningful information, and contribute alternative points of view. Thus, gray literature is utilized as background for this book. Far from being unreliable or questionable, the use of gray literature provides information that might not otherwise be available. As Eiteljorg (2008) pointed out, unpublished, uncatalogued, and limited circulation information is valuable in its own right. The University of New Mexico has pointed out that gray literature can include dissertations and theses, proceedings from conferences, reports, newsletters, technical notes, white papers, working papers, and others (Libguides: Gray Literature 101: Introduction, 2019, Examples). Carnegie Mellon University suggested that gray literature contains a great deal of information relating to studies that have not been posted, information that for one reason or another has not been formally announced, or even studies that were conducted which did not have a "significant effect" of one type or another ("Libguides: Systematic reviews: Conducting, finding and appraising: Searching the gray literature," 2019, para. 2). Yet, it can be just as important to know what research failed or was abandoned, or which ideas did not bear fruit. Thus, even if the gray literature reveals that an idea was considered and abandoned, it can be important for future research to be able to document that the idea was rejected or that research disproved it.

Although this is a qualitative project, the research is, at some points, described in terms of numbers of opinion. The number of opinions written per year or per administration may be considered, as well as the number of opinions overruled (by the President or Attorney General) or challenged in court, relative to the average length of service for either OLC attorneys or the Assistant Attorney General in charge of the OLC. The OLC has published 32 volumes of selected opinions that were written between 1977 and 2008. A 33rd volume of supplemental opinions covering selected opinions written between 1933 and 1977 was also published in 2013. It is unclear what percentage of the total number of opinions is included but Volume 1 does state that 25 percent of the opinions for that year are included. According to a Brennan Center for Justice report, 1,191 opinions were published between 1977 and 2009. The Sunlight Foundation found that 39 percent (201 out of 509) were not published for opinions written during the 1998–2012 time period (Schuman & Sahar, 2018).

There have been several lawsuits in recent years trying to force the OLC to release more opinions, using the Freedom of Information Act, by special interest groups such as the American Civil Liberties Union (most recently in 2012), the Citizens for Responsibility and Ethics in Washington (in 2013), and the Campaign for Accountability (in 2017). In what appears to be a response to these legal actions, the OLC has created a FOIA electronic reading room on its website where 130 memos, letters, and advice letters that were not previously selected for publication can be found. There are also two administrative and miscellaneous documents that discuss Best Practices for OLC opinions and two lists of OLC opinions for two separate time periods (1998–2013 and 2014–2016, with information redacted in both time periods). It should be noted, however, that this data relates to known documents, and to decisions that it is known were not published, up until the date this book was written. There is no way at this point to be certain that there were, or were not, additional opinions or what they were. The lawsuits that were mentioned may, or may not, bear fruit; and additional opinions may or may not be released or discovered. For this reason, any statistical analysis will be utilized in descriptive fashion and will not rise to the level of mixed or quantitative research.

Crabtree and Miller (1999, 7) suggested that certain types of research styles are better suited to some types of research questions and research aims. When the aim is identification, for example, the researcher will be asking *what is this, who is involved,* or *what is important*? The appropriate research style would then be a field investigation, or a documentary/historical approach. If the aim is to describe something (perhaps a trend), then the researcher will be asking *what is going on here? What dimensions exist in the concept that is being formed? What kind of variations on the theme might exist? What meanings or practices can occur that are linked to lived experiences*? These questions, which deal with the aim of describing what is going on, can also be answered with field investigation, or a documentary/historical approach (Crabtree & Miller, 1999, 7).

Normative descriptions, which address the value of the phenomenon, can be answered with field research, or a documentary/historical approach (Crabtree & Miller, 1999, 7). As the researcher seeks to explain what is happening and interpret patterns in either the phenomena or in what has occurred, he or she seeks to interpret what is going on, explain what is happening, and generate a description of the phenomena. The researcher may ask *what is happening, what patterns exist,* and *how do the phenomena relate to each other*? He or she asks *how are they different, how does the entire process work,* and *how did this occur or happen*? (Crabtree & Miller, 1999, 7). These questions are also typically answered with field work or a documentary/historical approach.

Each of these questions, taken separately, would provide valuable information and insight into the world of the Office of Legal Counsel and how it operates. Taken together, the questions form a framework of inquiry that guided the researcher in the investigation process. Table 2 reflects the questions that will be explored in this project.

A significant amount of reflection is involved in a project of this magnitude. The process began with reflection, and allowed the researcher to think about his history, and how he, and others in his field, was impacted by actions of the OLC. The questions that would be used in the researcher were drafted; data collection began; the data was organized and analyzed, and the thesis, which has since grown into a

Table 2. Questions Explored in This Project

Goal	Analysis	The Questions	The Style of Research
Identifying the phenomena	Identifying what is going on	What is this? Who is involved? What is important?	Field investigation, or documentary/historical investigation
Describing the phenomena	Describing what is occurring	What is going on here? What dimensions exist in the concept that is being formed? What kind of variations on the theme might exist? What meanings or practices can occur that are linked to lived experiences?	Field investigation, or documentary/historical investigation
Determining a normative description and explaining the situation	Determining what is right or wrong, or what the value of the phenomena is and how it relates to other facts	What is happening? What patterns exist? How do the phenomena relate to each other? How are they different? How does the entire process work? How did this occur or happen?	Field investigation, or documentary/historical investigation
Reflecting on the process	Determining the impact of the phenomena	How did these phenomena affect the researcher? How has it impacted other people? Why is this phenomenon so important from a wholistic standpoint?	Reflection, analysis of data that was collected, production of final report (i.e., book)

Source: Adaptation from Crabtree and Miller (1999, 7).

book, was produced. The end result, it is hoped, will be to provide the reader with a historical view of the OLC and the insight into why the organization is so important. If the reader understands why the OLC is so important, then they will be able to better understand the Office of the President, the workings of the Executive Branch, and the significance of many of the actions that are at the forefront of the political machine today.

Outline of the Book

The book is divided into twelve chapters. Each chapter addresses a different period in the history and operation of the OLC. Each of the chapters, except for the first chapter, concentrates on the administration of a particular President. The book is presented in chronological order, beginning with the inception of the Executive Adjudications Division, the precursor of the OLC, within the administrations of Franklin Roosevelt and Harry S. Truman.

Chapter 1—Origins and Background of the OLC

The first chapter of the book provides general background materials and an introduction into the operation of the OLC. The organizational structure of the Justice Department and the OLC is investigated, and the functions of the OLC are reviewed. The functions of the OLC focus on constitutional questions/issues, executive orders, and defending the administration of the various presidents in court. The OLC and its position in the Justice Department plays a significant role in the President's operations. This is particularly evident when society in America has gone through periods of social upheaval. The OLC is essentially the lawyer to the President and to all of the agencies that form the executive branch agencies. When the Attorney General releases a legal opinion, it has been carefully drafted by the OLC. The OLC plays a heightened role whenever a legal issue is particularly complex, or when agencies of the federal government are in disagreement. Whenever legislation is pending, the OLC is responsible for reviewing it and ensuring that the legislation falls within the bounds of constitutionality.

When the President has decided to issue an executive order or a significant proclamation, these documents must be reviewed by the OLC not only for legality, but also for form; in order to ensure that an order will hold up to legal scrutiny and not be challenged for a minor technical issue, the document must be carefully drafted, contain no confusing or incorrect information, and follow the form defined under the law. The OLC serves not only as counsel for the Executive Branch, but reviews orders and regulations that will need to be reviewed by the

Attorney General or that have been produced for the Attorney General's approval. In addition, the OLC will perform additional assignments that may have been given by the Attorney or Deputy Attorneys General.

Chapter 2—Franklin D. Roosevelt and Harry S. Truman Administrations

In 1934, the Office of Legal Counsel was created under a reorganization of executive branch agencies during the presidency of Franklin D. Roosevelt (1933–1945). The organization was originally headed by an assistant solicitor general, which suggests that Roosevelt may not have realized the importance that the organization would eventually have to the government of the United States. The original name of the OLC was the Executive Adjudications Division, and the Division was to participate in the important constitutional and legal issues of the era. Prior to 1951, the organization was headed by an assistant solicitor general. In 1951, however, Attorney General J. Howard McGrath changed the title of leader to assistant attorney general in charge. As the Executive Adjudications Division, the organization helped advise the President on the legal implications of the New Deal, World War II, Japanese internment orders, the court packing plan, the Truman Doctrine, Steel Seizure Cases, the Korean War, and the military desegregation executive order (which occurred under President Harry S. Truman). Chapter 2 includes a discussion of the important people involved in the early years of the agency, and the early role of the organization within the executive branch or national government.

Chapter 3—Eisenhower Administration

In 1953, Attorney General Herbert Brownell Jr. issued an administrative order changing the name of the Executive Adjudications Division to the current name, the Office of Legal Counsel, and giving the control of the organization to an individual he titled Assistant Attorney General in Charge ("Office of Legal Counsel," 2016). The Eisenhower administration faced a number of critical constitutional issues. The Cold War had started, and the nation was in the middle of the Red Scare. In May of 1954, the Supreme Court delivered its ruling in Brown v. Board of Education, which found that to segregate public schools was a civil rights violation; it violated the 14th Amendment.

In 1957, Eisenhower issued his Doctrine, which held that any country in the Middle East could ask for help from the United States (either financial or military) if it was faced with armed aggression. The Doctrine was partly in response to perceived threats by the Soviet Union. By issuing the Doctrine without specifically mentioning the Soviet Union, Eisenhower intended to send a strong message. The Eisenhower Administration provided the OLC with a great deal of material.

Chapter 4—Kennedy and Johnson Administrations

Chapter 4 discusses the role and evolution of the OLC in the important events of the Kennedy and Johnson Administrations. This was a time of great upheaval, both internationally and on the domestic front. Chapter 4 discusses the Bay of Pigs, Cuban Missile Crisis, Great Society, the Civil Rights Movement, and the Vietnam War.

Chapter 5—Nixon and Ford Administrations

This chapter focuses heavily on the Nixon Doctrine, foreign policy, Vietnam, the Affirmative Action executive order, and both Watergate and its aftermath. The aftermath of Nixon's pardon included requesting a decision from the OLC on matters relating to presidential or legislative pardons for presidents. This matter affected both Nixon (as the president who resigned) and Ford (as the president who might be awarding a pardon). In addition, the chapter pays special attention to the leadership of future Chief Justice William Rehnquist during this era.

Chapter 6—Carter Administration

President Jimmy Carter's administration focused on the energy crisis, Iranian hostage crisis, and the Soviet invasion of Afghanistan. In addition, OLC provided input into the Carter Doctrine, a policy intended to keep U.S. enemies out of the Persian Gulf. Each of these issues are investigated in the book.

Chapter 7—Reagan and George H.W. Bush Administration

Chapter 7 will focus on foreign policy issues that were plentiful in the Reagan and Bush administrations. The OLC was also heavily involved in advising the Executive Branch on issues relating to the foreign policy (especially relationships with countries in the Middle East), the War on Drugs, and criminal justice. Each of these issues is discussed at length.

Chapter 8—Clinton Administration

In 1998, articles of impeachment were instituted against President William (Bill) Clinton. The articles of impeachment were based on prior advice from the OLC relating to advisability of presidential impeachment, issued originally in 1973 and regarding impeachment of President Richard M. Nixon. This chapter will also focus on the role of the OLC in the line-item veto, in the case of Clinton v. Jones, health care reform, Clinton doctrine, and foreign policy.

Chapter 9—George W. Bush Administration

Chapter 9 will focus not only on role of the OLC in the War on Terror but on the presidential response to the terror attacks of September 11, 2001. The treatment of those captured and the response by the Department of Justice (torture memos) will be a focal point. Other topics of interest include physician assisted suicide and the Emoluments Clause.

Chapter 10—Obama Administration

High levels of activity during the Obama administration led to extensive actions by the OLC. Chapter 10 focuses on the Affordable Care Act (also referred to as Obamacare), gay marriage and marriage equality, the War on Terror, and on a wide variety of foreign policy achievements.

Chapter 11—Trump Administration

Chapter 11 focuses on executive orders produced early in Trump's administration, including opinions of the OLC relating to the travel ban relating to refugees, immigrants, non-immigrants, and green-card holders from specified Muslim-majority countries. Three travel bans were eventually issued, and the issue was addressed by the Supreme Court in September 2019. The book will be particularly timely relating to this issue, because there are expected to be significant developments between the initial stages of the book and the final book manuscript. The importance of the OLC and its opinions relating to these issues and to the future of America and America's immigration policy cannot be underestimated. There will be additional topics that evolve during the production of this manuscript, and chapter 11 will be updated accordingly.

One thread that evolved throughout the course of the book was OLC advice relating to impeachment, beginning with President Richard M. Nixon, reaching through impeachment actions of President William Clinton, and impeachment of President Trump. While it remains to be seen what will occur with a second impeachment action relating to President Trump, the OLC had been kept busy providing legal opinions into investigation of Trump's actions, actions of the FBI, and legal issues relating to impeachment actions. Thus, this topic will be continued from chapters 5 and 8.

Chapter 12—Conclusions

The final summation of how the OLC has performed its functions and evolved with passing administration is addressed in chapter 12. The role of the OLC is compared by considering how each presidential administration viewed its work, as well as the degree of influence the OLC had during each applicable era. The concluding chapter discusses the ways that the OLC has impacted American politics, and it considers the possibilities for operation of the OLC in the future.

Notes

1 Harvard Law Review 2008; see also the discussion of the OLC in Chapter 12 of this document.

2 Although the current orders are numbered, there is no single available master list accounting for the numbers or topics. Thus, it is impossible at the present time to

determine with any level of accuracy what the orders really were, how many there were, or even what they were about. It is likely that the OLC keeps a list that it does not allow the public, or even other agencies to have access to. This might be remedied in the future.

References

"Executive orders disposition tables index." (2019). *National Archives*. https://www.archives.gov/federal-register/executive-orders/disposition.

"Libguides: Gray literature 101: Introduction." (2019). *Libguides.Health.Unm.Edu*. https://libguides.health.unm.edu/graylit.

"Libguides: Systematic reviews: Conducting, finding and appraising: Searching the gray literature." (2019). *Guides.Library.Cmu.Edu*. https://guides.library.cmu.edu/c.php?g=586398&p=4050795.

"Office of Legal Counsel." (2016). *Allgov.Com*. http://www.allgov.com/departments/department-of-justice/office-of-legal-counsel?agencyid=7437.

"Organization, mission & functions manual: Attorney General, Deputy and Associate." (2014). *Justice.Gov*. https://www.justice.gov/jmd/organization-mission-and-functions-manual-attorney-general#ag.

"Organization, mission and functions manual."(2012). *Justice.Gov*. https://www.justice.gov/jmd/organization-mission-and-functions-manual.

"Organization, mission and functions manual: Office of Legal Counsel." (2014). *Justice.Gov*. https://www.justice.gov/jmd/organization-mission-and-functions-manual-office-legal-counsel.

"Truman executive orders disposition tables." (2019). *National Archives*. https://www.archives.gov/federal-register/executive-orders/truman.html.

Cover, A. (2012). Supervisory responsibility for the office of legal counsel. *The Georgetown Journal of Legal Ethics, 25*, 269–315. https://scholarlycommons.law.case.edu/cgi/viewcontent.cgi?article=1597&context=faculty_publications.

Crabtree, B., & Miller, W. (Eds.). (1999). *Doing qualitative research*. Thousand Oaks, CA: Sage.

Department of Justice. (2018a). Office of Legal Counsel. Last modified November 28, 2017. https://www.justice.gov/olc.

Department of Justice. (2018b). Office of Legal Counsel: Best practices for OLC legal advice and written opinions. Last modified July 16, 2014. https://www.justice.gov/olc/best-practices-olc-legal-advice-and-written-opinions.

Department of Justice. (2018a). Office of Legal Counsel: FOIA electronic reading room. Last modified November 8, 2017. https://www.justice.gov/olc/olc-foia-electronic-reading-room.

Department of Justice. (2018b). Office of Legal Counsel: Opinions. Last modified June 5, 2016. https://www.justice.gov/olc/opinions-main.

Eiteljorg, H. (2008). Grey literature: An obvious candidate for online access. *CSA Network, 21*(1). Accessed September 7, 2019, http://csanet.org/newsletter/spring08/nls0803.html.

Forrester, N. A. (2013). *Supplemental opinions of the office of legal counsel of the United States Department of Justice* (Vol. 1). Washington, DC: Government Printing Office. https://www.justice.gov/olc/file/477221/download.

Garrison, A. (2012). The role of the OLC in providing legal advice to the commander-in-chief after September 11th: The choices made by the Bush Administration Office of Legal Counsel. *Journal of the National Association of Administrative Law Judiciary, 32*(2), 648–718.

Garrison, A. (2013). The opinions by the attorney general and the Office of Legal Counsel: How and why they are significant" *Albany Law Review, 76*(1), 217–245.

Garrison, A. (2020). Phone interview with author. May 27, 2020.

Johnsen, D. (2004). Functional departmentalism and nonjudicial interpretation: Who determines constitutional meaning? *Law and Contemporary Problems, 67*(3), 105–148. https://www.repository.law.indiana.edu/cgi/viewcontent.cgi?referer=https://www.google.com/&httpsredir=1&article=1332&context=facpub.

Johnsen, D. (2006). Guidelines for the president's legal advisors (including principles to guide the office of legal counsel. *Indiana Law Journal, 81*(4), 1344–1354. https://www.repository.law.indiana.edu/cgi/viewcontent.cgi?article=1511&context=ilj.

Klaidman, D. (2006). Palace revolt. *Newsweek*. https://www.newsweek.com/palace-revolt-113407.

Lavitt, J. (2010). The crime of conviction of John Choon Yoo: The actual criminality in the OLC during the Bush administration. *Maine Law Review 62*(1), 155–198.

Liptak, A. (2019). Supreme Court says Trump can bar asylum seekers while legal fight continues. *Nytimes.Com*. https://www.nytimes.com/2019/09/11/us/politics/supreme-court-trump-asylum.html.

Morrison, T. (2010). Stare decisis in the Office of Legal Counsel. *Columbia Law Review, 110*(1), 1448–1525.

Morrison, T. (2011). Libya, hostilities, the office of Legal Counsel, and the process of executive branch legal interpretation." *Harvard Law Review, 124*(7), 62–74.

Yoo, J. (2007). *War by other means*. New York: Grove/Atlantic, Inc.

Yoo, J. (2008). *The powers of war and peace: The constitution and foreign affairs after 9/11*. Chicago: University of Chicago Press.

Chapter Two

Franklin D. Roosevelt (1933–1945) and Harry S. Truman (1945–1953) Administrations

Background

In 1934, the Office of Legal Counsel was created under a reorganization of executive branch agencies during the presidency of Franklin D. Roosevelt (FDR) (1933–1945). The organization was originally headed by an assistant solicitor general, which suggests that Roosevelt may not have realized the importance that the organization would eventually have to the government of the United States. The original name of the OLC was the Executive Adjudications Division, and the Division was to participate in the important constitutional and legal issues of the era. Prior to 1951, the organization was headed by an assistant solicitor general.

During FDR's administration, there were six different Assistant Attorneys in charge of the OLC: Angus D. MacLean (1933–1935), Golden W. Bell (1935–1939), Charles Fahy (1940–1941), Oscar S. Cox 1942–1943), Hugh B. Cox (1943–1945), and Harold W. Judson (1945–1946).

Selected Memorandum Opinions under Roosevelt

The cases that follow were selected because of their importance, or because they show the evolution of the development of interpretation of Constitutional law in the nation's earlier years. Many of these opinions are still in use today, and some have been interpreted by the Supreme Court.

Gold Clause

The Gold Clause cases are some of the most important cases the Office of Legal Counsel, in its early iterations, had to deal with. The decisions handed down in the Gold Clause case made the difference between currency that is backed by gold, and the use of script as currency. Between 1933 and 1935, Angus D. MacLean's period of service, the individual in charge of what would become the OLC was referred to as the Assistant Solicitor General. While MacLean handled several cases within the administration, the most important case was the "Gold Clause" which required the federal government to pay off all of its bonds, notes, and securities in gold. MacLean asserted that the government had the right to pay them off in any form of currency it chose, other than gold. This case was important at the time because to require the government to continue to pay its debts in gold would have completely depleted the nation's gold supply. This was in effect the first time the government tried to do away with the gold standard.

In April 1933, Roosevelt signed an executive order requiring all Americans to give their gold to the government. The reason for this, as Roosevelt insisted in a "fireside" chat, was that by turning all the gold over to the government and sticking with paper, all citizens would be put on the same footing, and the general welfare will be preserved (Roosevelt, 1933). Roosevelt, in this fireside chat, reminded citizens that a week after the inauguration, he had brought the banking crisis to everyone's attention. Two months later, he reported, the country was dying. Banks were going under, and mortgages were being foreclosed. Indeed, he comments:

> These institutions, because of their great needs, were foreclosing mortgages, calling loans, refusing credit. Thus, there was actually in process of destruction the property of millions of people who had borrowed money on that property in terms of dollars which had had an entirely different value from the level of March 1933. That situation in that crisis did not call for any complicated consideration of economic panaceas or fancy plans. We were faced by a condition and not a theory (Roosevelt, 1933: para 3).

Roosevelt (1933) continued with his explanation; as part of the plan to secure America, he was creating the Civilian Conservation Corps. Easing the public debt, building projects on public land, and authorizing the sale of beer in whatever states desired to do so were all part of the plan to "add to the comfort and happiness of hundreds of thousands of people" (Roosevelt, 1933: para. 8). Roosevelt's actions relating to the gold supply were somewhat ironic; in 1932, during the election, Herbert Hoover had tentatively suggested that it might be time for the US to abandon the gold standard. Roosevelt reacted very strongly, even calling the very possibility "a libel on the credit of the United States" (D'Amato, 2017: para. 3). Still, not far into his administration, here he was, and the groundwork had been set for four of the most important cases of the time.

Although the Gold Clause Cases, were heard, and decided in 1935, the best explanation of them at the time occurred in 1937 after MacLean had left the office. It was MacLean, however, who supervised the preparation of the Government's position in all four of the cases (MacLean, 1937). The arguments were actually made by MacLean's supervisor, Attorney General Homer Cummings. The four cases referred to as the Gold Clause cases were either heard directly in the Supreme Court or where certified by the US Court of Claims in Washington and sent to the Supreme Court to answer. In addition, there were a number of other cases that were in smaller courts across the United States and did not make it to the Supreme Court. Two of the cases involved the issue of bonds; the other two involved the gold clause which required payment in gold coins or the equivalent. Issues related to the Gold Clause all came from Public Resolution No. 10 of the 73rd Congress.

The Resolution had declared gold clauses void. However, it also enlarged the provisions of the Agricultural Adjustment Act of May 12, 1933 and made gold clauses to include coins and all currency of the United States, as well as of the debts and obligations, whether they were private debts between people and companies, or whether they were public (MacLean, 1937). The Resolution was particularly important for two reasons: first, it prohibited the use of gold clauses. Second, it declared gold clauses to be contrary to public policy. When something is contrary to public policy, it is not illegal per se, it is simply declared to be bad for the nation as a whole.

MacLean estimated that the number of obligations outstanding at the time of the Resolution were approximately 100 billion USD, while there were only 4 billion USD in the United States (and indeed, only 11 billion USD in the entire world). If the gold clauses were maintained, the dollar would be devalued or the value of gold content would be reduced, meaning that every dollar of debt would be increased to $1.69, enough to cause mass bankruptcy, even a national bankruptcy or collapse (MacLean, 1937).

Roosevelt believed that there were only two solutions; one was to let things happen as they may; the other was to develop policy that would put everyone on the same financial footing. He chose the latter, because it was "not only justified but imperative to our national security" (Roosevelt, 1933: para. 5). MacLean chose to proceed with the case, representing the Government, because he felt it "rested on broad constitutional grounds." He argued that Congress had power to coin money as well as to regulate its value, to regulate the use of foreign coin, and to determine what was legal tender. He pointed out that in the Civil War, the Legal Tender Acts made greenbacks legal tender for debts that were privately initiated, which gave precedent to the changes that President Roosevelt was proposing.

The Gold Clause is notable for another reason; it was considered to be very controversial because it marked one of the few times that the Court varied from the orders and interpretation that already existed. The dissenters to the decision argued that it killed the Constitution (D'Amato, 2017). For his part, Roosevelt felt very strongly about this decision, to the point that he had decided he would follow his conscience, even if it meant that he had to defy the Supreme Court.

Pocket Veto Case—3/16/1934

On March 16 of 1934, MacLean delivered a letter of opinion that addressed the issue of whether a three-day recess by one chamber of congress constitutes an adjournment for purposes of the pocket veto clause (Seitz, 2013). MacLean could find no real answer to this question. He did suggest that if the word "adjournment" were used then it clearly would be classified as an adjournment; otherwise, he suggested that the President should simply disapprove the bill and return it to the organization that originated it, thereby sidestepping the issue. MacLean did admit he had not run the question past the Attorney General, who at that time was Cummings.

Constitutionality of Law Conferring Einstein a Citizenship—4/09/1934

On April 9, 1934, J.T. Fowler, Jr., the Attorney-Adviser of the Office of the Assistant Solicitor General, reported that Congress did indeed have the authority to pass a law that granted citizenship to Albert Einstein. Fowler justified this opinion based on the Constitution, Article I, Section 8, Clause 4 (Fowler, 1934). After describing a number of times Congress had exercised this right, and a number of ways that citizenship could be conferred, Fowler closed with this comment: "Of course, it may be unwise to admit Professor Einstein to citizenship, and I have found no case of the admission of an alien under precisely similar circumstances" (Fowler, 1934).There are other cases in the records where the OLC give advice, but then states, in essence, that just because the president can do something surely does not mean he should

Exercising the Pocket Veto—6/26/1934

On June 26, 1934, MacLean provided a memorandum for the White House on exercising the pocket veto, as a follow on to the March 15 memo. In this memo, MacLean provided the opinion that if the President wanted to disapprove a bill, and it could not be returned because Congress was adjourned, Then instead of following the normal procedure for veto, the President should use a pocket veto. The normal course of action would be for a President to sign the bill but to endorse it by putting the word "disapproved" on it. This was the procedure established in the Constitution, art. I, § 7.

Legality of an Executive Order Making Requirements of Certain Departments—09/25/1934

In this decision, on September 25th, 1934, Homer Cummings, the Attorney General, had reviewed a request by the acting Director of the Budget, working with the Secretary of the Treasury, which would require all executive departments of the government to issue a statement of their assets and liabilities, every month, and to see that their report came out on the Daily Statement of the United States Treasury. The purpose was "to determine more readily and accurately the financial condition of the government" (Cummings, 1934, 1). As Cummings pointed out in his decision, once again the regulations in question were not authorized by statute. However, it was Cummings's opinion that since the President was the Chief Executive, he would have the authority to issue this type of order. Not only did the proposed regulations not limit or control the discretionary powers of the executive officers, but they would allow the President to make better executive-level decisions because he would have more data available. As Cummings suggested, the President was defined by the Constitution as needing to take care that the law of the United States was faithfully executed, and this order would help him do so. Cummings corrected some errors in form of the order, and then approved the revised draft, returning it for signature.

Removing the Assistant Secretary of Commerce 6/10/1935

MacLean's final memorandum opinion, dated June 10, 1935, addressed the legalities of the removal of the Assistant Secretary of Commerce by the Appointment of a Successor. MacLean's considered opinion was that the removal of the Assistant Secretary could be handled quite expeditiously simply by having the President appoint a successor, and then getting the Senate's approval. The President had asked the Assistant Secretary to voluntarily resign, but he declined to do so. MacLean presented several cases that were of similar findings; all had concluded that new officials could be nominated, and if approved by the Senate, would simply replace the incumbent (MacLean, 1935).

Other Memorandum Opinions under Roosevelt

In 1936, Golden Bell, MacLean's successor, was asked to determine the procedure for filling a vacancy following the death of the Secretary of War. This seemingly straight-forward issue was more complex than it appeared; the issue was that anyone appointed to the position on a temporary basis, which would have been Roosevelt's preference, could only serve for 30 days. It was not even clear if the President could temporarily take over the Secretary's work while a successor was being approved. After much consideration of the issues involved, Bell advised that any appointment should be a permanent one (Bell, 1936). The President made a permanent appointment based on Bell's verbal comments, causing Bell to decide that there was no need for a formal opinion. Rather, his memorandum was considered simply to be for the Attorney General's information.

Many of the cases that were handled in the early days of the OLC were simply clarifying points of law and were considered simply to ensure no Constitutional rules were being broken. Others, however, had further reaching implications, such as the censorship of transmission of Trotzky's speech from Mexico. Roosevelt had asked Bell to determine whether or not it was possible to censor Trotzky's telephonic speech from Mexico City to New York City. Bell's points very valid, and very telling politically. First, the Federal Communications Commission had no authority to censor telephone communications. Second, anyone who sought to interfere with the authority of the United States or to assist in a rebellion could be put in prison for 10 years and fined $10,000. Bell concluded that in this particular case, Trotzky's speech did not reach the level of inciting rebellion. His recommendation, therefore, was to use diplomatic relations to get the transmission stopped (Bell, 1937a).

In one of the longest opinions of the time, Roosevelt asked Bell to determine what his powers were in the field of foreign relations. After much background information, Bell informed the President that If there was an invasion or an imminent likelihood of attack, then the President had the power to take immediate action. Otherwise, he asserted, Congress did not intend that the President should hold all the power (Bell, 1937b). This issue has, of course, been in the news for the terms of several recent presidencies.

Other issues of the Presidency included whether or not the President could appear in criminal court as a character witness (no precedent) (Townsend, 1938), and whether or not the President had the authority to order the original Constitution be removed from the Library of Congress (no, by statute) (Bell, 1939b). In July 1939, the Office of Legal Counsel was asked to define the duties and procedures of the OLC, which it did (Bell, 1939a).

Wartime Memoranda

The remainder of Roosevelt's administration saw the OLC providing answers to questions of war, including whether or not members of the Naval Intelligence Service could conduct wiretapping (generally, no) (Jackson, 1941), or did the President control wireless and cable information that was leaving the United States (somewhat) (Fahy, 1941), and whether or not Japanese aliens and citizens could be taken from Hawaii and put in the continental US (most of the time) (Cox, 1942b).

Roosevelt's Final Years

Over the final three years of Roosevelt's Presidency, the opinions remained tied to war: trials of newspaper personnel who were accused of disclosing secrets (Cox, 1942c), and criminal liabilities for the newspapers that published those secrets (Cox, 1942a), appointing foreign agents without senate consent (Eberly, 1943), and even implementing civil aviation agreements with foreign aircraft (Eberly, 1945). These opinions were all consistent with a strong and nearly omnipotent federal government.

Memorandum Opinions under Truman

Truman became President 82 days into his vice presidency for Franklin D. Roosevelt, when Roosevelt passed away suddenly. He remained in office from April 12, 1945 to January 20, 1953. George T. Washington, Abraham J. Harris, and Joseph C. Duggan served as Assistant Attorneys General for the OLC. The first case considered under Truman's presidency was reinstatement of a federal judge following military service. In this case, the opinion was rendered that if a federal judge leaves to go to war, he cannot come back without a new appointment (Judson, 1945). This opinion is not consistent with what might be expected from the government of someone who voluntarily gave up a career to support the nation.

In general, the memorandum opinions under Truman related to recovery after the war and getting back to "business as usual," although by the end of his presidency, the Cold War was developing, and the nation was becoming concerned with the possibility of nuclear attack. This was becoming more obvious as school children practiced duck-and-cover drills, beginning in the 1950s following nuclear testing by the Soviet Union in 1949 (Pruitt, 2019). At the same time, the nation was still finishing the business of the last war, and governmental appointments ranged from the appointment of Justice Robert Jackson to prosecute Axis war criminals in Europe (he had the right to do so) (Clark, 1946) to the authority of Florida police to make arrests based on a notice from the FBI. In general, the government's rights or the President's wishes were upheld. However, in the case of Florida law enforcement, the finding was that even though the federal agencies had issued a pickup warrant, if it would constitute arresting someone without reasonable suspicion, then law enforcement did not have to comply. The memorandum so reflected and suggested that if this was not acceptable to the President then it would be appropriate to push for a change of law. This is a clear case of state's rights and a clash with federal law; the OLC went with states' rights on this issue. This issue began in the Truman presidency; the opinion was handed down a few days after the inauguration of Eisenhower (Rankin, 1953).

Conclusions

The Roosevelt years began with concerns relating to the stability of the economy and the removal of the requirement that debt be paid with gold. Subsequent decisions were related to war and the details of actions could, and could not, legally be taken by a standing president. By the time Truman came into office, the nation was largely getting back to its normal business, and the requests for clarification by the OLC reflected this new reality. With the advent of the Florida law enforcement case, the infancy of states' rights was highlighted. In the next chapter, the Eisenhower Administration is covered. The name of the Executive Adjudications Division is officially changed to the Office of Legal Counsel, and the Director is changed to Assistant Attorney General in Charge ("Office of Legal Counsel," 2016).

References

Bell, G. (1936). Filling the vacancy following the death of the secretary of war. *Justice Department*. https://www.justice.gov/file/20651/download.

Bell, G. (1937a). Censorship of transmission of Trotzky speech from Mexico. *Justice Department*. https://www.justice.gov/file/20656/download.

Bell, G. (1937b). The president's power in the field of foreign relations. *Justice Department*. https://www.justice.gov/file/20661/download.

Bell, G. (1939a). Jurisdiction and procedure of the office of the Assistant Solicitor General. *Department of Justice*. https://www.justice.gov/file/19196/download.

Bell, G. (1939b). Presidential authority to order the removal of the original engrossed Constitution from the Library of Congress. *Department of Justice*. https://www.justice.gov/file/20671/download.

Clark, T. (1946). Presidential appointment of Justice Robert Jackson to prosecute Axis war criminals in Europe. *Justice Department*. https://www.justice.gov/file/20621/download.

Cox, O. (1942a). Criminal liability for newspaper publication of naval secrets. *Justice Department*. https://www.justice.gov/file/20691/download.

Cox, O. (1942b). Removal of Japanese aliens and citizens from Hawaii to the United States. *Justice Department*. https://www.justice.gov/file/20681/download.

Cox, O. (1942c). Trials of newspaper personnel accused of disclosing naval secrets. *Justice Department*. https://www.justice.gov/file/20696/download.

Cummings, H. (1934). Legality of an executive order requiring executive departments and independent establishments to make monthly financial reports. *Justice.Gov*. https://www.justice.gov/file/19181/download.

D'Amato, D. (2017). The gold clause cases. *The Future of Freedom Foundation*. https://www.fff.org/explore-freedom/article/gold-clause-cases/.

Eberly, W. (1943). Presidential appointment of foreign agents without the consent of the Senate. *Justice Department*. https://www.justice.gov/file/20891/download.

Eberly, W. (1945). Implementation of international civil aviation agreements. *Justice Department*. https://www.justice.gov/file/20701/download.

Fahy, C. (1941). Presidential control of wireless and cable information leaving the United States. *Department of Justice*. https://www.justice.gov/file/20676/download.

Fowler, J. (1934). Constitutionality of legislation to confer citizenship upon Albert Einstein. *Justice.Gov*. https://www.justice.gov/file/19176/download.

Jackson,. (1941). Wiretapping by members of the naval intelligence service. *Department of Justice*. https://www.justice.gov/file/20886/download.

Judson, H. (1945). Reinstatement of afederal judge following his service in the army. *Justice Department*. https://www.justice.gov/file/20706/download.

MacLean, A. (1935). Removal of the Assistant Secretary of Commerce by the appointment of a successor. *Department of Justice*. https://www.justice.gov/file/20646/download.

MacLean, A. (1937). Outline of the gold clause cases. *North Carolina Law Review, 15*(3). http://scholarship.law.unc.edu/ cgi/viewcontent.cgi?article=1412&context=nclr.

Opinions of the Office of Legal Counsel of the United States Department of Justice, Vol. 3, 2007. (2014). Washington, DC: Office of Legal Counsel.

Pruitt, S. (2019). How 'duck-and-cover' drills channeled America's Cold War anxiety. *History.Com*. https://www.history.com/news/duck-cover-drills-cold-war-arms-race.

Rankin, J. L. (1953). Authority of Florida Police Officers to make arrests on the basis of FBI pick-up notices. *Justice Department*. https://www.justice.gov/file/20726/download.

Roosevelt, F. (1933). Outlining the new deal program – May 7, 1933. *Docs.Fdrlibrary.Marist.Edu*. http://docs.fdrlibrary.marist.edu/050733.html.

Seitz, V. (2013). *Opinions of the Office of Legal Counsel of the United States Department of Justice, Vol 1*. Washington, DC: Office of Legal Counsel.

Townsend, N. (1938). Presidential appearance as a character witness. *Justice Department*. https://www.justice.gov/file/20666/download.

Chapter Three

Eisenhower Administration 1953–1961

Background

In 1953, Attorney General Herbert Brownell Jr. issued an administrative order changing the name of the Executive Adjudications Division to the current name, the Office of Legal Counsel, and giving the control of the organization to an individual he titled Assistant Attorney General in Charge ("Office of Legal Counsel," 2016). The Eisenhower administration faced a number of critical constitutional issues. The Cold War had started, and the nation was in the middle of the Red Scare. In May of 1954, the Supreme Court delivered its ruling in Brown v. Board of Education, which found that to segregate public schools was a civil rights violation; it violated the 14th Amendment. This case is discussed briefly, not only because of its importance to the United States of today, but also because of its importance in the general unrest of Eisenhower's time.

In 1957, Eisenhower issued his Doctrine, which held that any country in the Middle East could ask for help from the United States (either financial or military) if it was faced with armed aggression. The Doctrine was partly in response to perceived threats by the Soviet Union. By issuing the Doctrine without specifically mentioning the Soviet Union, Eisenhower intended to send a strong message. The Eisenhower Administration provided the OLC with a great deal of material. Eisenhower's legal counsels included J. Lee Ranking, W. Wilson White, Malcolm R. Wilkey, and Robert Kramer.

Selected Memorandum Opinions under Eisenhower

The beginning of the Eisenhower administration saw the states' rights opinion related to Florida law enforcement and their right to follow Florida law, rather than a federal request, for the pickup of a fugitive. This case was discussed in chapter 2. In the next opinion, the government had sought the OLC's opinion on whether or not they could legitimately provide legal representation for members of Congress who were being sued civilly. Rankin (1953) proposed that the Attorney General's office could only represent members of Congress if it was in the best interest of the United States to do so, but in general, members of Congress could be represented if the department chose to do so, and it would depend on the department's policies (Rankin, 1953).

Balanced Budget 8/16/1955

In 1955, one of the first proposals for a balanced budget was submitted by Representative Cannon. The OLC's opinion was that to require the President to provide a balanced budget would be to limit the President's right to have enough money to finance the cost of such programs as might be required to run the government adequately, enumerated in 31 U.S.C. § 11(d) (1950) (Ford, 1955). In addition, Article II Section 3 of the Constitution states that the President must ensure that laws which have been enacted are executed. To require a balanced budget might infringe upon that requirement by limiting the available funds (Ford, 1955). The request for a balanced budget still comes up regularly, particularly as elections approach.

Public Land Availability for National Defense 7/12/1956; 2/24/1958

In the first opinion, the question was whether or not it was Constitutional for the President to use public lands for training and deployment purposes in the time of war, for national defense purposes (Rankin, 1956). In that opinion, Rankin pointed out that the issue had, to some extent, already been heard in the Supreme Court. The President as the commander in chief was allowed to do whatever he felt required to stabilize and support the armed services *in time of war*, without interference. Without a war, the decision would be left up to Congress. In the second opinion, Wilkey (1958) confirmed, again, that any changes to public law would require a provision for the President to be able to use public lands for military use under the Emergency Powers provision.

Authority to Blockade Cuba 1/25/1961

Shortly before Eisenhower left office, the OLC was asked to provide an opinion as to whether or not the President would have the authority to blockade Cuba. The response delivered by Kramer (1961, 195) was given mere days after Kennedy took office. The response was essentially a warning:

> ...the President is authorized to institute a blockade as an incident to a state of war. However, a blockade is a belligerent act which, as a matter of international law, is ordinarily justified only if a state of war, legal or de facto, exists.

This memorandum opinion will be discussed at greater length in the chapter relating to Kennedy, as it was President Kennedy who ultimately took action on the memo.

Other Memorandum Opinions under Eisenhower

It was during Eisenhower's time that the Cold War was ramping up. Cuba was becoming an issue. The United States was beginning to see the possibility of another war although it was not clear where the war would take place. There were a number of questions that attempted to determine the limits of the President's power, or in protecting perceived executive privilege by high-ranking government officials, particularly the Chairman of the Atomic Energy Commission (Evans, 1956). Evans advised that the Chairman's works and ideas were completely privileged, and he could not be compelled to testify or to release working papers, even if there was a question of fraud. Again, the specter of the Cold War loomed, and this particular memorandum reinforced the concerns of Americans as a whole of their safety in a nuclear world. Within a year the OLC was asked the same question about various independent regulatory agencies and gave the same response (White, 1957). In essence, the President was testing the limits to determine which of the Executive Staff could be compelled to testify as to what was occurring in the upper echelons of the government.

Brown v. Board of Education, 347 U.S. 483 (1954)

Although not a case advised by the Office of Legal Counsel, this case had a dramatic impact not only on people in the time of Eisenhower's leadership, but to this day. It is included not only because of its general importance but because of its importance in the politics of the day. In addition, it is very difficult to believe that the OLC did not, in some way, provide an opinion on a case of this importance. It is inconceivable that at some point the case was not discussed with the Attorney General, Assistant Attorney General, or staff of the OLC.

In 1951, thirteen families filed suit against the Board of Education in the City of Topeka, Kansas, in the State District Court for the District of Kansas. At the time, the law in Kansas, like much of the country, allowed school systems to set up segregated or separate schools for Black and White children. Children had to attend a school for their color even if it were further away. One of the families who filed suit, the plaintiff Oliver Brown, was chosen to represent the name of the suit. His young daughter had to catch a bus six blocks away to go to a "Black" school a mile away, even though there was a "White" school a block past the bus stop. The thirteen families filed to have their children allowed to go to the local school, but they were rejected and told to go to the "negro" school.

When the suit was heard in District Court, it was found in the favor of the Board of Education, citing *Plessy v. Ferguson*, 163 US 537, 539 (1896) in which the US Supreme Court had upheld the right of states to establish separate but equal facilities. In the original finding of Brown v Board of Education, the judge ruled that he believed that segregation was detrimental, but that the Topeka schools had been able to provide "separate but equal" facilities and education and thus were within the bounds of law at the time. However, when the case was appealed, a number of cases that had been filed in Virginia, South Carolina, Kansas, Washington, DC, and Delaware, were selected, and merged with the original Brown, because they had a common legal question relating to segregation. Again, Brown was chosen to be the name on the roster.

Brown vs Board of Education was chosen as the lead case for one important reason: Black schools in Topeka, Kansas were the closest in equality to White schools, in all of the jurisdictions represented. The Court was making a genuine effort to choose a case where the schools were as close to equal as possible, and Topeka (i.e., Brown) represented that chance. In the end the Court completely rejected the idea that facilities could be separate and equal. By the very definition, separate facilities are not equal, within the educational context. Racial segregation simply bred inequality and in addition to providing a weaker education, separate schools were detrimental to mental health of Black students. Segregation violated the Equal Protection clause.

The follow-on case to this one, *Brown v. Board of Education II* (1955) ordered the nation to desegregate with "all deliberate speed," which came to be known as one of the most famous phrases from American History.

Conclusions

Although Eisenhower was essentially a moderately conservative Republican, he was effectively elected because politically conservative voters across the United States were getting more and more concerned about the state of the world and hence their own survivability. Church membership even rose, and the Pledge of Allegiance had "under God" added to it, while new currency had "In God We Trust" printed on it (Black, 2018). On the home front, Eisenhower was modernizing society, including enforcing Civil Rights and Integration. The political arena around Eisenhower was becoming more and more nervous; Rosa Parks had refused to give up her seat in 1955, sparking a bus boycott and the threat of major violence. Privately, many of the members of the House and Senate were worried about what would happen if Blacks were given rights. It took military intervention to enforce *Brown*. In the United States, J. Edgar Hoover of the FBI believed that the civil unrest caused by Black activism could be exploited by the Soviet Union to gain power (Black, 2018). Overseas, Eisenhower declined to allow American troops to intervene in problems in Europe and the Suez Canal. In the next chapter, Kennedy's interactions with the Office of Legal Counsel and his place in the developing history of the United States are reviewed.

References

31 U.S.C. § 11(d) (1950).

Black, J. (2018). Eisenhower and the Cold War. *Foreign Policy Research Institute*. https://www.fpri.org/article/2018/02/eisenhower-cold-war/.

Brown v. Board of Education, 347 U.S. 483 (1954).

Brown v. Board of Education II, 349 US 294 (1955).

Evans, J. D. (1956). Assertion of executive privilege by the Chairman of the Atomic Energy Commission. *Justice Department*. https://www.justice.gov/file/20901/download.

Ford, F. (1955). Constitutionality of a joint resolution requiring the president to propose a balanced budget every year. *Department of Justice*. https://www.justice.gov/file/20736/download.

Kramer, R. (1961). Authority of the President to blockade Cuba. *Justice Department*. https://www.justice.gov/file/20756/download.

Plessy v. Ferguson, 163 US 537, 539 (1896).

Rankin, J. L. (1953). Authority of Florida Police Officers to make arrests on the basis of FBI pick-up notices. *Justice Department*. https://www.justice.gov/file/20731/download.

Rankin, J. L. (1956). Constitutionality of pending bills restricting the withdrawal of public land for national defense. *Department of Justice*. https://www.justice.gov/file/20741/download.

White, W. W. (1957). Applicability of executive privilege to independent regulatory agencies. *Justice Department*. https://www.justice.gov/file/20746/download.

Wilkey, M. (1958). Constitutionality of enrolled bill restricting the withdrawal of public land for national defense. *Justice Department*. https://www.justice.gov/file/20751/download.

Chapter Four

John F. Kennedy (1961–1963) and Lyndon B. Johnson (1963–1969) Administrations

Background

Chapter 4 discusses the role and evolution of the OLC in the important events of the Kennedy and Johnson Administrations. This was a time of great upheaval, both internationally and on the domestic front. Chapter 4 discusses the Bay of Pigs, Cuban Missile Crisis, Great Society, the Civil Rights Movement, the Voting Rights Act, the War on Poverty, and the Vietnam War.

During Kennedy's administration, there were two Assistant Attorneys in charge of the OLC: Nicholas Katzenbach (1961–1962), and Norbert Schlei (1962–1966). Schlei served under both Kennedy and Johnson. Schlei was replaced with Frank Wozencraft in 1966 and served until 1969.

Selected Memorandum Opinions under Kennedy

Authority to Blockade Cuba 1/25/1961

Days after Kennedy took office, Kramer (1961) provided the response of the OLC to the question as to whether or not the President had the authority to blockade Cuba. The response was essentially a warning to Kennedy that in the absence of a clear and present act of war on Cuba's part, Cuba would be able to take the United States to court over the action. It is clear at this point that Kennedy and Eisenhower would have discussed what was happening in Cuba, in the context of the presence of the Soviet Union in Cuba. School children were already doing air raid drills; America was afraid. Kramer suggested that in a worst-case scenario, Cuba and other nations might interpret a blockade in the absence of war as an act of war. If they did not respond by going to the International Court of Justice (or trying to) then they might interpret the blockade as an act of violence and take a defensive stance.

Intervention by States and Groups in Affairs of Another State 4/12/1961

In this opinion, Katzenbach argues that a nation that allows attack on another nation by a third party within its borders, allows an army to attack through its territories, or allows armed forces from another nation to train inside its border it is a violation of international law. Katzenbach did state that the neutral nation could allow the stockpiling of arms, and even allow volunteer soldiers from another nation to train there, provided they were not as organized as a real military force (Katzenbach, 1961).

The combination of these two decisions gives an insight into what was going through Kennedy's mind from the very beginning of his presidency. Combined with his question as to the potential role of the vice president, it appears that he not only was all too aware of international tensions and the intent of the Soviet Union but may have been concerned for his own safety. By seeking to allow Johnson more action at the executive level he may have been trying to ensure that if something happened, Johnson would be fully capable of taking over. The first memorandum of the new year considered the admissibility of wiretapping; Katzenbach (1962) advised that Congress was allowed to delegate regulation of wiretapping to the states. Again, this fits into the scenario of worry relating to the situation with the Soviet Union.

Authority to Take Action over Soviet Missile Bases 8/30/1962

The next two decisions, provided in August and October of 1962 , address the right of the President to take action under international law "if" the Soviet Union built missile bases in Cuba. The second question addresses the legal and practical consequences of blockading Cuba. The question about blockading Cuba had already been asked and answered, and it is unclear why Kennedy posed the question again.

Schlei (1962), who was presumably not privy to the details of the problems with the Soviets, stated that if it should occur that the Soviets really had built a base in Cuba, it would be permissible to take extreme measure to protect the United States and terminate or prevent the threat to the entire western Hemisphere. However, he pointed out, the United States would only be allowed to use as much force as necessary to protect its people.

The final memorandum in 1962 was unusual in that it was unsigned and was a repeat of a previous question. The answer was the same as when the question was asked previously. The President could establish a blockade, without Congressional action; however, depending on the outcome the United States might be questioned by the United Nations. Further, Cuba could regard it as an act of war (Unknown, 1962). This memorandum is worth reading for the historical content and also for the information relating to efforts to identify the author.

Within four days of the issuance of the last memorandum, Kennedy publicly confirmed that there were indeed Soviet missiles in Cuba (John F. Kennedy Presidential Library, 2019). Until that point, Kennedy had tried to keep it secret that the United States was aware of the missile site. He discussed the issue with advisors, received the unknown document described above, and decided to blockade. The final two memorandums of Kennedy's administration are of little interest to the subject at hand and thus will not be discussed.

Selected Memorandum Opinions under Johnson

Johnson was sworn in as President within minutes of Kennedy's assassination on November 23, 1963. He immediately faced the aftermath of the assassination, the investigation, the drama of the Bay of Pigs and the Cuban missile crisis, and the horror of the public. At the same time, Rosa Parks was still on the populace's mind, and the nation was desegregating under the order of Brown II. Johnson's first memorandum was in 1964 and addressed the use of federal personnel to deal with civil disobedience in Mississippi during the civil rights movement.

Katzenbach (1964) responded to Johnson that he had the authority to use federal troops in Mississippi but should do so only to investigate and prosecute federal crimes. He also stated that if there was a complete breakdown of law and order due to the Klan's presence or the presence in the Klan of large numbers of law enforcement personnel:

> ...the President could, as a legal matter, invoke the authority of sections 332 and 333 of title 10 to use military troops in Mississippi. There is considerable information available that could be used to support that assumption as to some areas in Mississippi (Katzenbach, 1964, 493).

Katzenbach also cautioned Johnson that presence of federal forces could make the problem worse if the local populace felt invaded, or if the police felt ostracized. Instead, he suggested, using marshals or FBI agents "strategically placed" would be a better idea. Katzenbach used the remainder of the memorandum to identify problems that needed to be solved.

Conclusions

The remainder of Johnson's administration was accomplished with little input from the Office of Legal Counsel. The three times that the OLC did provide him with responses, they were merely questions of daily operations. Johnson appears to have sought other advice for problems relating to the civil rights movement, to the war in Vietnam, and to voting concerns but those opinions are mostly not available because they have not been released or are considered classified. In the next chapter, Nixon and Ford are considered.

References

"Opinions." (2019). *Justice.Gov.* https://www.justice.gov/olc/opinions?f%5B0%5D=-field_opinion_post_date%3A1961.

John F. Kennedy Presidential Library. (2019). Cuban Missile Crisis. *JRK Library.* https://www.jfklibrary.org/learn/about-jfk/jfk-in-history/cuban-missile-crisis.

Katzenbach, N. (1961). Intervention by states and private groups in the internal affairs of another state. *Justice Department.* https://www.justice.gov/file/20771/download.

Katzenbach, N. (1962). Authority of congress to regulate wiretapping by the states. *Justice Department.* https://www.justice.gov/file/20786/download.

Katzenbach, N. (1964). Use of marshals, troops, and other federal personnel for law enforcement in Mississippi. *Justice Department.* https://www.justice.gov/file/20911/download.

Kramer, R. (1961). Authority of the president to blockade Cuba. *Justice Department.* https://www.justice.gov/file/20756/download.

Schlei, N. (1962). Authority under international law to take action if the Soviet Union establishes missile bases in Cuba. *Justice Department.* https://www.justice.gov/file/20791/download.

Unknown. (1962). Legal and practical consequences of a blockade of Cuba. *Department of Justice.* https://www.justice.gov/file/20906/download.

Chapter Five

Richard M. Nixon (1969–1974) and Gerald Ford (1974–1977) Administrations

Background

This chapter focuses heavily on the Nixon Doctrine, foreign policy, Vietnam, the Affirmative Action executive order, and Watergate and its aftermath, including Nixon's resignation and eventual pardon. The chapter will pay special attention to the leadership of Rehnquist and Ehrlichman during this era. Ralph Erickson and Roger Cramton were also members of the OLC during Nixon's time. Despite the actions that led to Nixon's resignation, there were also many significant occurrences and societal changes in the Nixon era. These impacts will be briefly addressed as well. A great deal of attention has been paid to Nixon's tenure, because of the impact it had on later presidencies and national policy relating to impeachment and prosecution of the Executive Branch. For this reason, the chapter is significantly longer than the other chapters in the book.

From 1953 to 1961, Richard Milhous Nixon served as Vice President under Dwight Eisenhower, whose presidency was reviewed earlier in this book. Two incidents which impacted later history and involving Richard Nixon occurred during the time frame surrounding the Eisenhower presidency. The first had its roots in the 1950 Senate elections and was somewhat scandalous; the second occurred later, during the Eisenhower presidency itself. A third event, relating to potential impeachment of Nixon, was to have a great deal of impact on the impeachments of President Donald Trump .

Selected Memorandum Opinions under Nixon

Tricky Dick and the Checkers Speech

From 1948 to 1950, Richard Nixon was head of the House Un-American Activities Committee (HUAC). Nixon was rabidly anti-Communist; he pursued Alger Hiss, the former State Department Official, with an absolute vigor. While Hiss denied the charges that he was a communist and was spying for the Soviet Union, he also argued that he had never met his accuser, an individual named Whittaker Chambers. Nixon was able to get Hiss to admit that he knew Chambers in the past, but that Chambers had used a different name at the time. The result was a charge of perjury and five years of imprisonment. This incident gave Nixon a reputation as a hard-nosed anti-Communist. In 1950, when Nixon ran for the Senate, his opponent was Helen Douglas, an individual who believed the anti-Communist movement was morally wrong. Nixon retaliated by having his campaign staff distribute pink flyers that insisted Douglas's voting record was left wing. Nixon earned the nickname "Tricky Dick" as a result of this incident; the name followed him throughout his life and colored people's view of his personal morality.

Eisenhower, who was running for President, chose Nixon as his running partner because he felt that Nixon's dogged determination would be good for the party. However, only two months before the campaign, a major newspaper reported that they had discovered that Nixon's campaign donors had set up a private "slush fund" for Nixon to use for personal needs. At this point, Eisenhower began to receive pressure to release Nixon from the campaign ticket. It was Eisenhower's belief that if Nixon were not on the ticket, the Democrats would win the election. Thus, he decided to give Nixon time to clear his name and remain on the ticket.

Nixon's speech concentrated on the fact that he did not use money improperly; he pointed out that his wife had an inexpensive coat, not a fur coat like many of the Democratic wives. In the conclusion of the speech, Nixon did admit to accepting a political gift: a puppy for his daughter, who had named the dog "Checkers." While the speech was not expected to make a difference politically, the public loved the speech, which became known as the "Checkers Speech" ("Richard Nixon (1913–1994)," 2019). The OLC was forced to issue rules relating to the acceptance of gifts, as a guideline for the future. The Checkers speech had one clear effect, though: it gave Nixon a real distrust of the media. This distrust played into Nixon's actions towards the media, which will be discussed later in this chapter ("Opinions," 2019–2020).

Development of the 25th Amendment: Presidential Disability and Succession

Over the period from 1955 to 1957, Eisenhower's health took a turn for the worse. During this time period he experienced not only a heart attack, but a stroke. At the time, the position of the vice president had little real power ("Richard Nixon (1913–1994)," 2019). It was already understood that if a president died, the vice president would take his place. However, there was little to no provision for what would happen if a president became disabled but did not die. Nixon was able to take a strong position as Vice President and took over responsibilities for passing bills that Eisenhower had expressed concern about, including the Civil Rights Bill of 1957 ("Richard Nixon (1913–1994)," 2019). Eisenhower was concerned enough about his health and the nation that he worked with Nixon to develop a formal agreement on what powers and responsibilities vice presidents would have if their president became incapacitated.

Congress passed the Amendment in 1965 ("25th Amendment," 2019). In 1967, the plan for vice presidential responsibility in the event of presidential disability, which had been encompassed in the 25th Amendment, was formally adopted as an amendment to the

Constitution ("25th Amendment," 2019). This Amendment was to become critically important to the history of the nation on March 30, 1981, when President Ronald Reagan was shot by John Hinckley Jr. and Secretary of State Alexander Haig declared he was "in charge" (Purdy, 2015; Stathis, 1982). George H.W. Bush, who was in the air over Texas en route to an appointment, returned to the White House and took over as acting president (Purdy, 2015), even though there is evidence that the 25th Amendment was not formally invoked.

The OLC and Potential Impeachments

By 1973, there were several accusations against President Nixon that appeared to be leading to the possibility of impeachment. Perhaps the most impactful of all the actions to come out of the Office of Legal Counsel was penned on September 24, 1973, by Robert G. Dixon, Jr., the Assistant Attorney General for the Office of Legal Counsel, in response to inquiries regarding the "Amenability of the President, Vice President, and other Civil Officers to Federal Criminal Prosecution while in Office." Dixon's opinion for the OLC was to have far-reaching implications not only into the impeachment of President Bill Clinton, but also those of President Donald Trump.

Dixon was asked to opine on whether or not it would be possible to prosecute a sitting president or vice president for crimes, while that individual was in the offices to which he or she had been elected. Dixon's first comment was that this question had been a subject of debate since the very earliest days of the United States. Three specific questions were addressed: Whether the civil officers could be prosecuted for crimes before an impeachment was complete; if the answer was no, then to what extent the President could be held accountable to the federal courts as a potential defendant in a criminal case; and finally, if the President were found to be immune from criminal prosecution by virtue of being in office, would that immunity be shared by the Vice President, and to what extent (Dixon, 1973).

In answering the first question, Dixon reached back to the original Constitution, which addressed impeachment and prosecution in Article I, section 3, clause 7, which states:

> Judgment in Cases of Impeachment shall not extend further than to removal from Office, and disqualification to hold and enjoy any Office of honor, Trust or Profit under the United States: but the Party convicted shall nevertheless be liable and subject to Indictment, Trial, Judgment and Punishment, according to Law. ("Article 1 Section 3 Clause 7 Constitution," 2020)

According to Dixon, the goal of the clause was to prevent any argument that the President was subject to double jeopardy. By imposing criminal charges *after* impeachment was dealt with, it was believed that the double jeopardy argument could not be used. Dixon followed the arguments as far back as speeches that were given by Luther Martin, who had participated in the Constitutional Convention, and other early political pundits. After a great deal of analysis and discussion, Dixon concludes that the judiciary should be responsible for trying criminal offenses, and Congress would have jurisdiction over impeachment. However, it is important to note that a president or vice president does not have to be impeached in order to be charged with a crime. Dixon's analysis concluded that if the president had to be impeached in order to be charged with a crime, then Congress would feel pressured to impeach so that a criminal prosecution or even investigation could be begun. This would be ineffective in terms of both time and money.

For the second question, whether or not immunity of a President from a criminal trial could be justified for other reasons, Dixon reiterated that no immunity is conferred on the President. Pickney, a former member of the Continental Congress, argued that the omission of immunity was deliberate:

> ...if Congress possessed the power some gentlemen contend for on this point, they must previously legislate on it in the same manner. On this subject there can be no doubt of the propriety of this objection, if Congress possessed the power; and their never having passed such a law is a strong proof, that whatever opinions either branch may have entertained, that both did not suppose they possessed this power, or certainly they would have legislated on it. (*The Debates and Proceedings and All the Laws of a Public Natures; with a Copious Index 6Th Congress* 1851, 70–71, hereinafter The Debate)

If Pickney's argument is accepted, since Article I, Sec 6 Clause 1 provides for limited immunity of the legislative branch, then it could be said that the President is not entitled to any immunity by virtue of his position (Pickney, in The Debate, 70). Alexander Hamilton differed with this interpretation, however (Dixon, 1973). In the end, Dixon concludes that during the last century, the demands on a President have become so "onerous" that it would take away from his ability to be president if he had to defend against criminal prosecution; thus, only Congress should have the right to interrupt business this way, and the method was to be impeachment.

Dixon thoroughly investigated the position of the Vice President in determining whether or not the Vice President could be prosecuted, and determined that a Vice President should be indicted, in order to avoid any problems with the statute of limitations, especially since a delay would benefit any cited co-conspirators.

Additional Memorandum Opinions under Nixon

The cases that follow were selected because of their importance, or because they show the evolution of the development of interpretation of important laws. In general, these apply to the Nixon doctrine, a foreign policy that expected the Asian nations to tend to their own defense and went hand in hand with withdrawal from Vietnam. Nixon also took on Affirmative Action. Opinions of the OLC relating to Watergate and its aftermath of impeachment were discussed earlier in the chapter. Many of these opinions are still in use today, and some have been legislated through the Supreme Court ("Opinions," 2019–2020).

Effect of Repeal of the Tonkin Gulf Resolution

The Gulf of Tonkin Resolution or the Southeast Asia Resolution, Pub.L. 88–408, 78 Stat. 384 was enacted in August of 1964 in Johnson's administration. The resolution was a joint resolution by the House and Senate that allowed President Johnson to use military force in the Bay of Tonkin. By issuing a joint resolution, the legislature allowed the use of military intervention, without formally declaring war. By the time that Nixon was elected, the war in Vietnam was very unpopular and public opinion supported leaving Vietnam. In 1970, Nixon sought to determine what the effect of repealing the Tonkin Gulf Resolution would be. Richard Kleindienst delivered the opinion for the OLC. After carefully considering all the issues involved, he concluded that it would be impossible to determine the legal effect of repealing the Tonkin Gulf Resolution (Kleindienst, 1970). In summary, he felt that the Constitutional authority to deploy troops abroad depended on the circumstances of the deployment, the use of force necessary to protect Americans, and the use of force necessary to preserve American lives. Thus, there were simply too many variables to give an absolute response.

Authority to Enter Cambodia-Vietnam Border Area

On March 14, 1970, William Rehnquist issued a response to a request for a ruling on whether the President could authorize troops to enter the area of the Cambodian-Vietnam border. After consideration, Rehnquist concluded that since Congress had authorized the President to "take all necessary measures to protect U.S. troops in Southeast Asia" (1970, 313), the President would have authority to order entry into Cambodia-Vietnam border area if he felt it was necessary.

Destruction of Vietnamese and Cambodian Sanctuaries

A week after Rehnquist's response to the President's authority to enter the Cambodian-Vietnam border area, he issued a memorandum ruling whether the President had the war power to order invasion of South Vietnam and Cambodian sanctuaries (Rehnquist, 1970a). Rehnquist's decision spoke to the nature of the position of Commander in Chief. Provided, he stated, that the title conveyed authority to some degree over the armed forces, then the President had the right to make this tactical decision. He found that the Constitution designated the title of Commander in Chief to convey substantive authority, and thus the President had the right to authorize this decision (Rehnquist, 1970b).

Self-Pardon of a President

On August 5, 1974, the Office of Legal Counsel submitted its opinion on presidential or legislative pardon of a sitting President. Lawton (1974) found that the President could not pardon himself, because it was impossible for someone to be a judge in his own case. However, if a President were to declare that he was temporarily unable to do the jobs required of a president, the Vice President would be declared Acting President. Because he would hold the power of the office, he could then pardon the President. After this, the President could resign, or he could say that he was now able to do the job of President again (Lawton, 1974). It was only four days from this point that President Nixon resigned his position and stepped down from the presidency.

The events that led up to this decision and ultimately to Nixon's resignation centered around Watergate and the President's concerns that the media were dishonest. The problem began shortly after Nixon's State of the Union address on January 22, 1971. Within a month, Nixon had audio taping systems activated in the White House, and the Oval Office fitted with a voice activated system. The Cabinet Room had a manual system that Nixon or his assistants could activate ("Richard Nixon—Key events," 2019). By early April, Nixon was able to use voice-activated taping in the Executive Office Building, the Oval Office, and the Lincoln room. By mid-June, someone had leaked the "Pentagon Papers" to the New York Times. When they published these papers, the White House set up a group of "plumbers" to stop leaks in the White House. In mid-May, a voice-activated taping system in the lodge at Camp David was ready to use, as well as a system hidden in the Camp David study desk ("Richard Nixon—Key events," 2019).

In mid-June, police caught five individuals inside the Democratic Headquarters in the Watergate Hotel. The five individuals were armed with $2,300 in cash, cameras, and materials to set up a wiretapping system. Within a week, President Nixon had ordered his Chief of Staff, Haldeman, to tell the FBI that the Watergate investigation needed to be stopped on national security grounds. On August 23, 1972, Nixon got the Republican nomination for President. Less than a week later, he was forced to deny that his office had any involvement in the Watergate break-in. He won re-election and was inaugurated ("Richard Nixon—Key events," 2019).

On March 4, 1973, the voice-activated taping system and the desk telephone taping systems at Camp David were disabled. At the end of April, Nixon went on television and took responsibility for the Watergate affair, but denied that he knew about it before it happened. It was not until June 21, 1973, that telephone taping ended in the table phone at Camp David. The next month, the voice-activated system in the Oval Office was deactivated, and the head of the Federal Aviation Agency confirmed before the Senate Watergate Committee that taping had been taking place. However, it was two more days before the systems in the Oval Office, Cabinet Room, Lincoln Room, and the Executive Office Building were terminated. When the Committee subpoenaed the tapes, Nixon claimed executive privilege and refused to provide the committee with the tapes. At this point, Nixon took to the airwaves again and denied any involvement in the Watergate incident. Within two months, Spiro Agnew, the Vice President, had resigned under pressure for taking campaign contributions in return for contract awards. When Agnew resigned, Congress confirmed Gerald Ford as Vice President on October 12, 1973 ("Richard Nixon—Key events," 2019).

Although Nixon attempted to carry on his job as President, the intervention of the Senate Watergate Committee was taking up more time. Over the next few months, Nixon refused to turn over subpoenaed tapes for "security reasons," refused to resign in the State of Union address and demanded that the investigation be stopped. The IRS investigated Nixon's taxes and asked for $432,787 in back taxes, along with $33,000 in fines. The pressure that he was under was immense. By the end of April 1974, Nixon had released over 1,200 pages of transcripts of his conversations.

During all of this timeline, the Supreme Court had been hearing arguments relating to Nixon's turning over of the tapes. In May 1974, Vice President Ford advised Nixon to give the House Judiciary Committee the information that they wanted. Nixon declined, and by the end of July, the Supreme Court had ruled, 8–0, to require Nixon turn 64 tapes over to the Senate Committee. These tapes were to show the level of Nixon's knowledge and complicity in the Watergate burglary.

Three days later, the Committee levied three articles of impeachment, including obstruction of justice, abuse of power, and defiance of subpoenas. Though Nixon complied with the order and released the tapes, the information contained was so problematic it would be impossible to recover. Nixon insisted he would not resign, although his friends and advisors were suggesting that he do so rather than lose the impeachment. He prevaricated only two days before he resigned on television on August 8, 1974. On August 9, 1974, Gerald Ford, the appointed Vice President, was sworn in as President. The Special Prosecutor who had been appointed insisted that he would continue the investigation and prosecution of the ex-president. Exactly one month after the resignation, the new President, Gerald Ford, pardoned Nixon, putting Lawton's 1974 OLC decision to good use.

Memorandum Opinions under Ford

Much of President Ford's term of office was spent rebuilding American trust in the American system of government. As a result, the questions posed to the OLC tended to be those which clarified day to day operations. The Constitutionality of the Federal Advisory Committee Act, December 1, 1974, did not reach any real conclusions. It served instead to present arguments for whether or not Congress could use its power to oversee or regulate committees that advised the President.

In 1976, the OLC reported on three issues: whether or not it would be constitutional to pass a bill creating an Office of Congressional Legal Counsel, whether not the Constitution permitted appointing a Federal judge to the United Nations, and whether or not it would be Constitutional to have regulatory reform legislation for independent governmental agencies. In all three cases the recommendation was made that the actions would be constitutional ("Opinions," 2019–2020).

Conclusions

The Nixon years were very tumultuous, with a wide variety of important acts from the standpoint of ending the war in Vietnam and improving the civil rights of Americans as a whole. Unfortunately, they were interspersed with illegal and immoral acts, in a partnership that brought down both the President and Vice President and set up an odd dynamic that saw Gerald Ford serving first as Vice President and then as President. However, the Nixon administration had a number of implications for Presidents of the future, including Clinton and Trump, and is notable for the number of importation clarifications of law that resulted.

References

"25th Amendment." (2019). *History*. https://www.history.com/topics/united-states-constitution/25th-amendment.

"Article 1 Section 3 Clause 7 Constitution." (2020). *Constitution.Congress.Gov*. https://constitution.congress.gov/browse/article-1/section-3/clause-7/.

"Executive orders disposition tables index." (2019). *National Archives*. https://www.archives.gov/federal-register/executive-orders/disposition

"Opinions." (2019). *Justice.Gov*. https://www.justice.gov/olc/opinions?f%5B0%5D=-field_opinion_post_date%3A1961.

"Opinions." (2020). *Justice.Gov*. https://www.justice.gov/olc/opinions?f%5B0%5D=-field_opinion_post_date%3A1976.

"Richard Nixon—Key events." (2019). *Miller Center*. https://millercenter.org/president/richard-nixon/key-events.

"Richard Nixon (1913–1994)." (2019). *Biography.Com*. https://www.biography.com/us-president/richard-nixon.

Dixon, R. G. (1973). Amenability of the president, vice president and other civil officers to federal criminal prosecution while in office. *Department of Justice*. https://fas.org/irp/agency/doj/olc/092473.pdf.

Kleindienst, R. (1970). Supplemental opinions of the Office of Legal Counsel in Volume 1: Effect of a repeal of the Tonkin Gulf resolution. *Justice.Gov*. https://www.justice.gov/file/20916/download.

Lawton, M. C. (1974). Presidential or legislative pardon of the president. *Justice.Gov*. https://www.justice.gov/file/20856/download.

Purdy, M. (2015). Who was in control of the government when Ronald Reagan was shot?—Presidential history. *Presidential History*. https://presidentialhistory.com/2015/05/hws-calmness-aftermath-reagan-assassination.html.

Rehnquist, W. (1970a). Presidential authority to permit incursion into communist sanctuaries in the Cambodia-Vietnam border area. *Justice.Gov*. https://www.justice.gov/file/20821/download.

Rehnquist, W. (1970b). The president and the war power: South Vietnam and the Cambodian sanctuaries. *Justice.Gov*. https://www.justice.gov/file/20826/download.

Schuman, D., & Sahar, A. (2018). 39% of Office of Legal Counsel Opinions kept from the public. *Medium*. https://medium.com/@danielschuman/39-of-office-of-legal-counsel-opinions-kept-from-the-public-f9c32055e6ab.

Stathis, S. (1982). Presidential disability agreements prior to the 25th amendment. *Presidential Studies Quarterly, 12*(2), 208–215. https://www.jstor.org/stable/27547806?seq=1.

The debates and proceedings and all the laws of a public nature; with a copious index 6Th congress. (1851). Washington, DC: Gales and Seaton.

Chapter Six

Jimmy Carter (1977–1981) Administration

Background

From January 20, 1977 to January 20, 1981, a gentleman peanut farmer from Plains, Georgia served as the President of the United States after defeating the incumbent, Gerald Ford. While President Carter tended to be a philosopher and philanthropist, his administration was a stressful one, focusing on the energy crisis, the Iranian hostage crisis, and the Soviet invasion of Afghanistan. The OLC was also asked to provide input into the Carter Doctrine, a policy intended to keep U.S. enemies out of the Persian Gulf. Altogether, President Carter was responsible for 320 Executive Orders, and the OLC had input into many of these orders. Due to the large number of memorandum opinions for this President, they will be discussed in general rather than in specific terms.

A General Discussion of Memorandum Opinions under Carter

The Presidential Transition Act's provision of services and medical corpsman to transitioning ex-Presidents was the first memo put to the OLC. At issue was what services and aircraft Carter could make available to former President Ford to ease his transition back into civilian life from what had been an unusual term of office. Leon Ulman issued the opinion for the OLC. Parts of the memorandum would have great applicability today. Ulman pointed out that any travel the first six months after transition, which can be linked to transition, whether personal or business, must be at no cost to the departing President, to "promote the orderly transfer of executive power" (Ulman, 1977, 319). It was Ulman's opinion that the incoming President could, if he desired, allow the departing President to use Air Force One, complete with a medical corpsman. The President could also appoint an aircraft to carry ex-President Ford, without a medical corpsman, on a one-time basis. Finally, if the Director of the Secret Service felt that it would be less expensive and safer, the head of the Secret Service could dedicate a military aircraft and a medical corpsman for six months, because this would be in line with the legal requirement to protect the outgoing President. It would also be less expensive for the federal budget.

The next memorandums were to clarify points that an individual who was more involved in national politics might already have known. Carter was not, however, a politician on the national or international level at his election, and wanted various conditions clarified for himself and the staff. Within two weeks, the OLC established that the law firm associated with a former US Attorney could not represent a corporation, and that volunteers could indeed work in the White House, despite federal labor laws ("Opinions," 2020). The OLC established that the Hatch Act allowed members of the White House Staff to continue to be members of the Democratic National Committee, and that there was a conflict of interest in dealing with litigation that involved a corporation that was owned by a former government attorney. Similar conflicts of interest when leasing planes for private or official use, or when former Justice Department attorneys want to appear in particular lawsuits were considered. By mid-February, the OLC was asked to determine whether or not a state legislature could take back its ratification of a Constitutional Amendment. The OLC felt that it could do so, provided there was a substantial change in the society or environment before the amendment would need to be ratified. Since there was only seven years left to ratify the ERA, the amendment in question, John Harmon, the OLC officer, felt that there was no reason the state should not be held to its original vote ("Opinions," 2020).

By mid-1977, the OLC had found that damage claims under the Atomic Energy Act could not be excluded and were involved heavily in litigation against R.J. Reynolds, the Tobacco Company. In this case, the President sought an opinion as to whether or not the federal government should be required to pay the expert witness fees for its own expert witnesses in US v. RJ Reynolds Tobacco Company. Ulman's memorandum emphasized that the court's rules required payments for expert witnesses, and Congress and the US Government was not excluded by this requirement ("Opinions," 2020). The next memorandum, unsurprisingly, was asked to establish which agency should be required to make that payment to expert witnesses in cases handled by the DOJ.

General Lack of Familiarity with Process

Through the year of 1977, the relatively routine nature of the questions submitted to the OLC reflected a lack of familiarity with process, rather than the need to address new situations or concerns. There were also numerous requests for rulings on retirement pay for specific individuals from a variety of agencies, what specific clauses in various Acts and administrative rulings applied to, and whether or not employees could represent family and friends in various hearings or intervene in various civilian situations.

One of the issues that John Harmon (1977c) opined related to gifts that were intended for the White House, the Vice President's residence, or the offices of the Vice President or President. The issue was related in a roundabout way to the question of emoluments that would arise in later presidencies. Harmon (1977c) pointed out that there is authorization under legislation for the ability to accept gifts of art and for furnishings that were intended for the official residences for the White House, the Vice President, or for the offices of the President and Vice President. He advised the President that all gifts accepted for this purpose would be taken under the control of the Secretary of the Navy (for the Vice Presidency) or the National Park Service (for the White House). The gifts, whether money or property, would be entered into the national accounting system and become part of the permanent property of the United States.

In May of 1977, Carter posed a request for opinion regarding the growth of the giant scarlet poppy, the *Papaver bracteatum*, to the Office of Legal Counsel. Carter's question was bifurcated: did the Drug Enforcement Administration (DEA) have the authority to control production of the plant and could growth or production of the plant be prohibited. In a nine-page response, Ulman (1977) opined that there were only two grounds that the federal government could use to prohibit production of the poppy (or any plant). The first would be if production of the plant would violate obligations of the US for various treaties, and the second would be if production of the plant would be inconsistent with the interests of the public (Ulman, 1977). Ulman concluded that if the DEA concluded that "controlled domestic production would result in a substantial increase in the supply of illicit controlled substances in the United States" then the government would have the right to declare that allowing any production at all would be against the public interest (1977, 98–99). Another possibility was established in the Single Convention, which would allow the government to allow the growth of a limited production of plants for the drugs that they could produce, rather than to prohibit their growth completely. This is the opinion that formed the basis of limitation for opium poppies, coca bushes, and cannabis plants, and laid the groundwork for the eventual War on Drugs.

Carter and his staff questioned everything from whether it was constitutional to allow employees to take time off to celebrate religious holidays (yes) to whether or not prison inmates had to be given due process before being transferred to administrative segregation (yes, except for emergencies). Ulman was even asked to determine what the phrase "dealing with more than one logically consistent subject matter" meant. Ulman opinioned that "logically consistent subject matter" referred to a broad purpose within government, or perhaps referred to different agencies that had similar purpose ("Opinions," 2020).

On September 8, 1978, Carter asked the OLC to determine whether the National Security Council had to be considered as an agency, for purposes of the Freedom of Information Act (yes). John Harmon wrote the decision, in which he states:

> NSC could be held to be an Agency by a simple, literal application of the language of 5 U.S.C. § 552(c). In our opinion, the better approach is to examine whether NSC is within the exception from inclusion stated in the conference report (1978, 205).

The large number of questions to the OLC asking for clarification as to whether a particular agency or condition would be subject to tort liability or legal liabilities of various kinds suggests that this presidency was acutely aware of the implications of all of the government's actions.

Still, there were many questions that reflect Carter's energy concerns. He asks, for example, if the government could put employment restrictions on ex-employees in the government's nuclear facilities and ensure that they did not take up particular jobs. Ulman's opinion was that the government could allow them to join civilian energy agencies but could put requirements on that employment ("Opinions," 2020).

Dealing with Iran

Although the first two years of Carter's Presidency seemed to be devoted to exploring the limits of government power, when the Iranian embassy in Tehran was seized, the situation changed. The tone of the requests to the OLC were vastly different than those of the first two relatively relaxed years. In the hours following the seizure, John Harmon drafted a memorandum for the Presidency Relating to the Situation in Iran (Harmon, 1979a). Harmon made the following recommendations to Carter: Block Iranian assets and stop oil traffic; stop export of American goods to Iran; restrict the movement of Iranian diplomats and send troops to protect Americans abroad. In the next memorandum, Harmon was forced to clarify that he did not mean for the President to arrest or detain Iranian diplomats; Carter could only detain them (Harmon 1979c).

During the remainder of the Carter Presidency, the OLC led Carter through implementing Emergency Powers, consideration of deporting the Shah back to Iran, limiting communications from Iran, and the

Shah of Iran's legal status. What to do with Iranian diplomats while staying within the bounds of both American and Iranian law became a strong consideration, as did the valuation of Iranian assets. Various non-military actions against Iran were considered, as well as the ramifications of litigation with Iran. The OLC also opined on the legality of seizing financial assets from Iran and what the likely ramifications would be. Finally, by September of 1980, the OLC was advising Carter on his authority to settle the crisis with Iran (Opinions, 2020). Throughout the entire next year, the OLC advised on various agreements with Iran, and Carter had issued the Carter Doctrine as a way of dealing both with Iran and the Soviet Union. By January 1981, however, the OLC was being asked to give an opinion as to whether or not the agreement with Iran that the President made was legal, and whether or not it would be possible to get out of the agreement ("Opinions," 2019–2020).

Selected Memorandum Opinions under Jimmy Carter

Role of the Solicitor General

Harmon (1977b) discussed the relationship between the Attorney General's office and the office of the Solicitor General (SG), as well as the role that each office should play when the Government is involved in litigation that is being presented to the Supreme Court. Both the Solicitor General's office and the Attorney General's office were created by legislative acts, in 1870 and 1789 respectively. The Attorney General's office was to prosecute suits before the Supreme Court, while the Solicitor General was to be an officer that would assist the Attorney General as he completed his tasks. According to statute, the Attorney General could require the Solicitor General to argue any case in which the AG believed the government had an interest. Harmon (1977b) concluded that the Solicitor General's position was designed to assist the AG. However, once the SG has made a legal decision or advice, the AG is to accept it unless the position is completely outside of the position of law. Harmon (1977b) advised the President that the AG should not intervene with the SG's position because there are other avenues with which an erroneous position could be reversed.

Congressional Access to Tax Returns

In May 1977, the Acting Commissioner of the Internal Revenue Service (IRS) sought the OLC opinion on whether or not Congress could have access to Federal tax returns and the tax return information. Harmon (1977a) found that Congress intended for the various subcommittees to be able to look at tax returns and the information on them. The question was under what conditions. The subcommittees were accustomed to asking the IRS directly, and Harmon (1977a) indicated this practice needed to stop. He concluded that the subcommittees could inspect returns and their information, but only if the committee chairman requested it and indicated why it was being requested, in conjunction with a particular inquiry. This was the only way access should be granted.

Removal Power or Disciplinary Action of Presidential Appointees—Constitutional Law

In 1978, the General Counsel for Civil Service and the General Counsel for the President's Reorganization Project queried whether they would have the power to remove a Presidential appointee who was performing functions appointed by the President. The Civil Service Commission Reform Bill (S 2640) was pending at the time. Hammond (1978) concluded that from a Constitutional standpoint, (Article II, § 2, cl. 2), Congress could not remove an appointee, nor could they discipline the appointee through demotion, suspension, or debarment. While the Constitution seemed to be open to reprimands and civil penalties, Hammond believed that taking this action would "cloud" the President's power base (1978, 109) and was thus not permissible.

Amending the Constitution by Convention

In January 1979, the Attorney General requested the OLC provide an opinion on whether or not the Constitution could be amended by convention. Hammond (1979b) asserted that the question had never occurred before. Thus, he commented, his decision was based on scholarly writing rather than law or case history. Based on the fifth article of the Constitution, which states that two thirds of the states have to vote to call a convention to propose amendments, it seems clear that the states could propose to change the amendments if they could not get Congress to propose them. The convention would not get a general meeting to propose amendments, but rather would meet to deal with *one* proposed amendment. The exception to this would be that if more than one state wished to propose similar amendments, Congress could aggregate them. The question exists as to whether or not the conclusion of the vote would require the President's approval. Hammond (1979b) concluded that this would likely be heard by the courts at some point.

Convention for Proposing Amendments

In October 1979, the Attorney General once again brought a question relating to Constitutional amendment to the OLC. This time the AG wished to know whether Article V of Constitution authorized a general convention process, or a limited convention process. Harmon (1979b) reviewed the issue at great length but concluded that "the meaning of the Convention Clause is simple and clear" (410). The consensus, he pointed out, could be either narrow *or* general. The Convention could even call for a complete overhaul of the Constitution. However, the 2/3 vote requirement of the states would have to be met in order for the convention to convene. Further, ratifying any action the convention took would need an "extraordinary majority of the governments of the States" (Harmon, 1979, 410). This would not, therefore, be an action to be undertaken lightly. Harmon included the Proceedings of the Convention of 1787 in Appendix I of his decision, a description of previous Congressional handling of applications for conventions in Appendix II, and the early applications of the states as Appendix III. The deadline for ratification of the Equal Rights Amendment (ERA) had been set as March 22, 1979. However, the ratification date was expanded to 1982, making the Attorney General's question quite pertinent.

Conclusions

Although Carter was essentially an untried individual when he became President, he did not hesitate to avail the OLC for legal advice. While Carter was dealing with the Iranian challenges, the Soviet Union attacked Afghanistan. Although he was not reelected, President Carter was awarded a number of awards, essentially for his humanitarianism under pressure. These included the Albert Schweitzer Prize for Humanitarianism in 1987, the United Nations Prize in the field of Human Rights in 1998, the Indira Gandhi Prize in 1997, the Presidential Medal of Freedom in 1999, and the Noble Peace Prize in 2002 ("Jimmy Carter quick facts," 2020). Many of the intense questions Carter's Presidency did not come from the Executive Office, but rather from General Counsels of various agencies.

References

"Jimmy Carter quick facts." (2020). *Jimmy Carter.* https://jimmycarter.info/president-mrs-carter/jimmy-carter-quick-facts-bio/.

"Opinions." (2019). *Justice.Gov.* https://www.justice.gov/olc/opinions?f%5B0%5D=-field_opinion_post_date%3A1961.

"Opinions." (2020). *Justice.Gov.* https://www.justice.gov/olc/opinions?items_per_page=10&order=field_opinion_post_date&sort=asc&f%5B0%5D=field_opinion_post_date%3A1977.

Hammond, L. (1978). Presidential appointees—Removal power or Disciplinary Action—Constitutional Law (Article II, § 2, Cl. 2). *Justice.Gov.* https://www.justice.gov/file/21566/download.

Hammond, L. (1979). Constitutional Law—Constitution—Article V—The amending process—The convention method. *Justice.Gov.* https://www.justice.gov/file/18351/download.

Harmon, J. (1977a). Congressional access to tax returns—26 U.S.C. § 6103(F). *Justice.Gov.* https://www.justice.gov/file/21036/download.

Harmon, J. (1977b). Role of the solicitor general. *Justice.Gov.* https://www.justice.gov/file/21201/download.

Harmon, John. (1977c). "Acceptance of Gifts to Be Used in the White House, the Official Residence of the Vice President, or the Offices of the President and Vice President". Justice.Gov. https://www.justice.gov/file/21326/download.

Harmon, J. (1978). Freedom of Information Act (5 U.S.C. § 552)—National Security Council—Agency Status under FOIA. *Justice.Gov.* https://www.justice.gov/file/21696/download.

Harmon, J. (1979a). Supplementary discussion of the president's powers relating to the seizure of the American Embassy in Iran. *Justice.Gov.* https://www.justice.gov/file/22316/download.

Harmon, J. (1979b). Constitutional convention—Limitation of power to propose amendments to the constitution. *Justice.Gov.* https://www.justice.gov/file/22181/download.

Harmon, J. (1979c). Presidential powers relating to the situation in Iran. *Justice.Gov.* https://www.justice.gov/file/22311/download.

Ulman, L. (1977). Presidential Transition Act (3 USC 102 Note)—Provision of military aircraft and hospital corpsman to a former president (31 USC 638). *Justice.Gov.* https://www.justice.gov/file/21291/download.

Chapter Seven

Ronald Reagan (1981–1989) and George H. W. Bush (1989–1993) Administrations

Background

From January 20, 1981 to January 20, 1989, a former Captain in the US Army turned actor became President of the United States. His time in office was to focus on the Cold War relationship with the USSR, the development of the Reagan Doctrine, Reaganomics, and the air traffic controller's strike. Reagan was also the victim of John Hinkley Jr., a would-be assassin who was determined to kill the President to impress a young actress. The administration was a stressful one, with George H.W. Bush stepping in to do the President's duties as he recovered from the attempted assassination that left Reagan's press secretary, James Brady, permanently disabled. In Chapter Five, the development of the 25th Amendment relating to Presidential disability and succession was reviewed. It was the 25th Amendment, developed in part by Nixon and Eisenhower to account for Eisenhower's poor health. The amendment created a mechanism for having an Acting President while an incapacitated President was recovering (25th Amendment, 2019). There is some evidence, however, that Bush did not want the 25th Amendment formally invoked.

Vice President George H.W. Bush was in the air over Texas, on his way to another meeting, when the shooting occurred. The Secretary of State, Alexander Haig famously declared he was "in charge" after Reagan's shooting (Purdy, 2015; Stathis, 1982), highlighting a lack of understanding of the functionality of the highest levels of the government. George Bush returned the next morning and began doing the President's duties (Purdy, 2015). The timing was particularly concerning given that the Soviet Union was poised to invade Poland. Reagan had only been President for 70 days at this point (Peppard, 2015). Reagan was hospitalized for 13 days.

George H.W. Bush was also a military officer, and he stepped into Reagan's place in March 1981, as well as on another occasion when Reagan was having colon surgery. Bush was heavily involved in the War on Drugs and the first Gulf War.

A General Discussion of Memorandum Opinions under Reagan

President Reagan began utilizing the OLC immediately after his inauguration. The first OLC decision related to the restructuring of the relationship between the federal government and Radio Free Europe (RFE). Leon Ulman (1981) issued the decision, advising Reagan that he could reorganize the financing given to RFE without Constitutional issues. The OLC had been asked to rule on whether or not there were separation of powers concerns caused by providing financing to RFE. Within a week, Reagan had asked the OLC to determine if he were allowed to direct agencies to postpone any regulations that might be scheduled to go into effect, for a 60-day period. The OLC opinion was that the President's office could direct agencies to dispense with the normal procedures if a new President was taking office in a period of economic instability or distress (Simms, 1981c). Reagan, of course, was taking office during a period of high economic distress.

Reagan requested the OLC to review the legal implications of implementing the Agreement with Iran that had been discussed by President Carter. It was Reagan's concern that a number of domestic legal challenges were going to arise from dealing with Iran, and he sought advice on the actions that he could and could not take. It is clear from the language in the OLC decision by Simms (1981b) that Reagan had asked what the repercussions of non-implementation of the agreement with Iran might be. The OLC opined that it would be possible to make a persuasive argument that the agreement with Iran was actually null and void under international law, as it was procured under the threat of force. Thus, the OLC reasoned, it could be argued that the agreement was actually void under the Vienna Convention on the Law of Treaties and the US, under the direction of a new president, would have the right to decide whether or not it wished to repudiate the agreement. Simms (1981b) did point out that if the United States decided to repudiate the agreement, there would be a number of concerns relating to the Iranian assets that had already been frozen pursuant to the agreement. On balance, however, the decision was strongly in Reagan's favor. A follow-up question the next month asked the OLC to determine whether or not it would be possible to treat the agreement with Iran as being partially acceptable but to hold other parts null and void. Simms (1981d) advised that, while there was legal precedent for holding some parts of the agreement void, Iran would undoubtedly retaliate. He strongly cautioned that "any breach of the agreement could set in motion a serious train of consequence" (Simms, 1981d, 333) and thus suggested that Reagan should take "great care" in considering what to do.

Sprinkled throughout Reagan's term in office were the typical administrative requests that every President encountered in the general course of doing the nation's business. Other issues, however, gave an indication of the direction the President would be taking with his office and with public policy. In March 1981, for example, the OLC was asked to advise on the constitutionality of allowing misdemeanor punishments to include sentences that exceeded a year. At issue was an amendment proposed to the Lacy Act, which could result in misdemeanor convictions of up to five years in prison if the individual convicted had been designated as a "special offender." Simms (1981a) advised the office of the President that the year's limitation on misdemeanor punishment was constitutionally based and thus could not be modified unless the constitutional provisions were respected. Thus, any extension of the conviction sentence would only be allowed if the grand jury had met and indicted; an "information" would not be adequate.

By the end of March 1981, the attempted assassination of Reagan had occurred and the OLC was asked to provide advice on delegation of power and presidential succession in the event of disability, the Attorney General's duty to defend the Constitution, and the constitutionality of statutes that would impose the death penalty for the assassination of the president ("Opinions," 2020).

In December 1981, Reagan asked the OLC for an opinion as to his powers with regard to Libya. The memorandum was written by Theodore Olson (1981). The memorandum was much more detailed than the one that had been written relating to the Iranian issues and provided Reagan with a very detailed list not only of suggestions but of the regulations and laws surrounding the activation of the options.

Reagan's OLC memoranda, like those of Jimmy Carter, reflect a very wide range of concerns. From questions about the Equal Rights Amendment to a request for a personal determination on retirement benefits from the State of California, Reagan did not hesitate to ask the OLC to intervene. Reagan even asked the OLC to provide advice on proposed changes that might be made to the witness protection program. In November 1982, Reagan took the proactive step of asking the OLC to provide him with an opinion of what steps he could take, and what legal authorities were available, should there be a severe energy reduction in terms of petroleum products (Opinions, 2020). The question of governmental privilege in response to a court order was readdressed; this is one issue that seems to be a regular thread throughout the presidencies.

In 1983, Reagan asked the OLC to provide an opinion as to whether an Assistant United States Attorney could be dismissed because he was homosexual. The OLC opined that even if homosexuality were against the law in some areas, the individual should be retained unless his performance was negatively impacted by his orientation.

Through the years of the Reagan Administration, the number of referrals to the OLC decreased on a yearly basis. In 1985, Reagan did ask for a number of clarifications regarding the 25th Amendment's implications for Presidential Succession ("Opinions," 2020).

Memorandum Opinions under George H.W. Bush

In George H.W. Bush's first year in office, he asked the OLC to confirm whether or not Posse Comitatus would apply outside of the United States territories. He also asked for the OLC to evaluate whether or not it was constitutional to require prior Congressional notification for CIA covert actions. Throughout the course of his time as President, Bush's attentions concentrated on legality of military actions, implications of actions of the FBI and assorted intelligence agencies, and, increasingly as his presidency progressed, the use of various federal assets, including drug dogs, for interdiction actions, aiding in civilian law enforcement, but also in aid of actions by the National Guard when used in Washington DC ("Opinions," 2019–2020).

During Bush's first year in office, many of the requests for OLC opinions dealt with typical administrative works. The constitutionality of Veterans' job training requirements, various personnel authorities of the Environmental Protection Agency relating to its employees, resolutions disapproving pay raises, cost of living allowances, and implications relating to the Clean Air Act were investigated. However, at the same time, Bush's politics were beginning to be reflected in the questions directed to the OLC. Several months into his Presidency, Bush asked the OLC to provide guidance on a question that had been addressed before – whether or not the Inspectors General would need to provide information on open criminal investigations to Congress, should they ask. Kmiec (1989) provided an extensive response; summarized, Inspectors General are not required to provide Congress with confidential information.

In the second half of 1989, Bush asked the OLC to provide input as to whether or not the FBI could be properly used to conduct background investigations for Congress (they can). Foreshadowing the War on Drugs, the OLC provided an opinion as to whether or not Customs Service could offer a reward for information leading to the location of individuals who had been indicted for drug trafficking (Barr, 1989a). Barr opined that various government offices could offer such rewards, but not Customs. One of the more important decisions related to the FBI's authority to override or ignore international or extraterritorial law in pursuit of law enforcement activities. The OLC's advice was that the FBI could conduct activities that were not in violation of US law, even if they were in violation of international law (Barr, 1989b). This decision was to have far reaching impact on both the war on drugs and anti-terrorism activities. In mid-1990, the president asked the OLC to determine whether or not the United States could lease (or loan) aircraft to other nations for use in narcotics interdiction. An extremely short opinion by Luttig (1990) concluded that narcotics control could be considered a defense action, and that the President had the authority to lend or loan aircraft for defense purposes.

Conclusions

Together, Reagan and Bush formed the nexus of very conservative years in the office of the presidency. Each man brought his own opinions and impressions of what was right and what was wrong into the White House. Peppard (2015) suggested that at one point, it was difficult for the two men to define their positions as being that of President and Vice President, as they were such good friends they were simply equals. This may be one reason that Reagan reportedly did not invoke the 25th Amendment when he was shot.

Throughout the Reagan and Bush administrations, a great many administrative circumstances were reviewed by the Office of Legal Counsel at behest of the respective Presidents. Some of the decisions are very clear-cut and in support of the President's viewpoints, while others are provided with a word of caution relating to the implications for the President or his staff. While some of the decisions are clearly one-sided, others are well-rounded and well-discussed. This is the issue that is important in a discussion of the OLC, and nowhere is it more obvious than in the presidencies of Reagan, the Bushes, and, later, Trump.

References

"25th Amendment." (2019). *History*. https://www.history.com/topics/united-states-constitution/25th-amendment.

"Opinions." (2019). *Justice.Gov*. https://www.justice.gov/olc/opinions?f%5B0%5D=-field_opinion_post_date%3A1961.

"Opinions." (2020). *Justice.Gov.* https://www.justice.gov/olc/opinions?items_per_page=10&order=field_opinion_post_date&sort=asc&f%5B0%5D=field_opinion_post_date%3A1977.

"Opinions." (2020). *Justice.Gov.* https://www.justice.gov/olc/opinions?f%5B0%5D=-field_opinion_post_date%3A1981&f%5B1%5D=field_opinion_post_date%3A1981-04.

Barr, W. (1989a). Authority of the customs service to offer rewards for information concerning the whereabouts of indicted drug traffickers. *Justice.Gov.* https://www.justice.gov/file/24231/download.

Barr, W. (1989b). Authority of the federal bureau of investigation to override international law in extraterritorial law enforcement activities. *Justice.Gov.* https://www.justice.gov/file/24241/download.

Kmiec, D. (1989). Congressional requests for information from inspectors general concerning open criminal investigations. *Justice.Gov.* https://www.justice.gov/file/24181/download.

Luttig, J. M. (1990). Lease or loan of aircraft to foreign countries for assistance in international narcotics control under subsection 506(A)(2) of the Foreign Assistance Act of 1961. *Justice.Gov.* https://www.justice.gov/file/23406/download.

Olson, T. (1981). Executive power with regard to the Libyan situation. *Justice.Gov.* https://www.justice.gov/file/22861/download.

Peppard, A. (2015). Tested under fire: How George H.W. Bush asserted control in the wake of the Reagan assassination attempt. *Dallas Morning News.* http://res.dallas-news.com/interactives/reagan-bush/.

Purdy, M. (2015). Who was in control of the government when Ronald Reagan was shot?—Presidential history. *Presidential History.* https://presidentialhistory.com/2015/05/hws-calmness-aftermath-reagan-assassination.html.

Simms, L. (1981a). Constitutionality of allowing punishment of misdemeanor by a sentence exceeding one year. *Justice.Gov.* https://www.justice.gov/file/22611/download.

Simms, L. (1981b). Review of Domestic and International Legal Implications of Implementing the Agreement with Iran. *Justice.Gov.* https://www.justice.gov/file/22426/download.

Simms, L. (1981c). Presidential memorandum delaying proposed and pending regulations. *Justice.Gov.* https://www.justice.gov/file/22581/download.

Simms, L. (1981d). Whether the agreement with Iran can be treated as void in part. *Justice.Gov.* https://www.justice.gov/file/22431/download.

Stathis, S. (1982). Presidential disability agreements prior to the 25th amendment. *Presidential Studies Quarterly,* 12 (2): 208–215. https://www.jstor.org/stable/27547806?seq=1.

Ulman, L. (1981). Restructuring the relationship between the federal government and radio free Europe/radio liberty. *Justice.Gov.* https://www.justice.gov/file/22576/download.

Chapter Eight

William Clinton (1993–2001) Administration

Background

William (Bill) Clinton was sworn into office on January 20, 1993 and turned the keys to the Oval Office over to George W. Bush, the son of George H.W. Bush, on January 20, 2001. Clinton's presidency concentrated on the line-item veto, health care issues, the Clinton Doctrine and foreign policy. Clinton also found himself dealing with the aftermath of inappropriate relationships with women other than his wife. The first well-known incident, which took place prior to Clinton's election, resulted in one of the more well-known court cases of the time, Clinton v. Jones, 520 U.S. 681 (1997). Clinton v. Jones, which went to the Supreme Court, established that a sitting president does not have immunity from civil litigation that resulted from acts that took place before taking office and which had no relationship to the office of the President.

The second case resulted in impeachment proceedings, with charges of lying under oath and obstructing justice. In the Clinton v. Jones case, Clinton had testified under oath that he had never had an affair with Monica Lewinsky, a young intern at the White House. However, in his hearing in front of a grand jury investigating his conduct, he acknowledged having the affair. The confession, which contradicted his testimony in Clinton v. Jones, led to impeachment action ("President Clinton's impeachment trial begins," 2020).

Selected Memorandum Opinions under Bill Clinton

Constitutionality of Health Care Reform

The OLC was asked to determine whether or not the Health Security Act was within the authority of Congress under the basis of the Commerce Clause, and whether or not it violated the Tenth Amendment. Walter Dellinger and H. Jefferson Powell delivered the opinion for the OLC. After examination of the issues, the OLC declared that the Health Security Act would give all citizens of the United States the security of having health care that would be readily and consistently available to them. According to the authors, adequate health care would help preserve the Federal system, would support the Constitutional rights of individuals, and was based on Constitutional principles that had been well-established. As a result, the OLC felt that the President, with the assistance of Congress, could establish both national and state health boards to begin to implement health care reform on the national level (Dellinger & Powell, 1993), a fight that continues to the time of this writing.

Deployment of US Armed Forces into Haiti

In May 1994, Clinton announced his intent to send American troops to Haiti to help restore the government of the elected President Jean-Bertrand Aristide (Freed, 1994). On July 31, 1994, the United Nations Security Council Issued Resolution 940 approving Operation Uphold Democracy. It was the first resolution issued to authorize the use of force to restore democracy (Carey, 1997). An invasion began on September 17, 1994, with several members of the Republican legislators threatening to take action to stop the invasion at the last minute, although they did not. Those legislators, however, did ask the OLC for an opinion on the legality of the action, which was duly issued on September 27, 1994. Walter Dellinger issued the OLC's opinion, stating that the President did have Constitutional Authority to deploy troops into Haiti and that the evidence showed the President had considered the action carefully before approving it (Dellinger, 1994). This action marked the beginning of continuing human rights interventions into other nations.

Balanced Budget Amendment

President Clinton was a strong supporter of the line-item veto as a way to help balance the budget and gain better control over the budget. However, in January 1995, Walter Dellinger of the OLC gave a statement before the Joint Economic Committee of the United States Congress in which he discussed the proposed Balanced Budget Amendment. It was Dellinger's opinion that other alternatives should be considered prior to trying to pass a budget amendment. He particularly suggested that line-item vetoes should be utilized in this process, as part of a way to reduce the deficit. He concluded by stating that the balanced budget should not be considered as an amendment because it was unattainable (Dellinger, 1995).

Summary of Additional Memorandum Opinions under Bill Clinton

President Clinton continued to follow issues related to his main emphases as President, asking the OLC to recommend whether or not he could deploy armed troops into Bosnia, and whether or not he had the discretion to postpone making determinations that would trigger sanctions under the Chemical and Biological Weapons Control and Warfare Elimination Act of 1991. He also asked the OLC to rule on whether or not legislation denying citizenship at birth to certain children born in the United States would be Constitutional. He also asked them to determine whether or not it was legal to seek assistance by state and local police during the process of apprehending illegal aliens, and whether or not he could legally restrict the import of munitions under the Arms Control Act. Shortly thereafter, the OLC was asked to provide advice on issues relating to the implementation of the Brady Act, which had been passed as a result of the injury of James Brady during the attempted assassin of President Reagan ("Opinions," 2020).

In 1996, Clinton's thoughts were deep; he approached the OLC with a request for information relating to the Constitutional separation of powers between Congress and the President. Like other Presidents before him, he sought advice in the area of Executive Privilege, in this instance regarding the White House Counsel's office documents. He also sought advice on placing the armed forces under the control of the United Nations control for operational or tactical operations. Over the last years of his presidency, Clinton continued to address issues relating to executive privilege in a number of different contexts. In particular, he sought the advice of the OLC on whether or not the Counsel to the President should be given immunity from compelled Congressional Testimony. The OLC responded that because the Counsel was one of the President's closest advisors, he would indeed be given immunity from testifying ("Opinions," 2020).

Conclusions

The Clinton years were an unusual mix of concern for the humanitarian needs of other nations and personal concerns in terms of the results that could occur from his own behaviors. Clinton found himself in the position of needing to consult previous OLC decisions relating to impeachment during Nixon's time. His advisors recommended that he weather the impeachment process, believing there was not enough evidence to warrant conviction. This is in direct contradiction to Nixon's advisors, who had recommended resignation. In the end, Clinton's advisors were right; there was not enough evidence for an impeachment conviction, and he finished out his term as President.

References

"Opinions." (2020). *Justice.Gov.* https://www.justice.gov/olc/opinions?items_per_page=10&order=field_opinion_post_date&sort=asc&f%5B0%5D=field_opinion_post_date%3A1977.

"President Clinton's impeachment trial begins." (2020). *History.* https://www.history.com/this-day-in-history/clinton-impeachment-trial-begins.

Carey, H. F. (1997). The UN humanitarian intervention in Haiti and the development of a human rights enforcement regime. *Journal of Haitian Studies, 3/4,* 30–47.

Clinton v. Jones, 520 U.S. 681 (1997) https://supreme.justia.com/cases/federal/us/520/681/.

Dellinger, W. (1994). Deployment of United States armed forces into Haiti. *Justice.Gov.* https://www.justice.gov/file/20306/download.

Dellinger, W. (1995). The balanced budget amendment. *Justice.Gov.* https://www.justice.gov/file/20261/download.

Dellinger, W., & Powell, H. J. (1993). Constitutionality of health care reform. *Justice.Gov.* https://www.justice.gov/file/20451/download.

Freed, K. (1994). Clinton to send troops to Haiti. *Baltimoresun.Com.* https://www.baltimoresun.com/news/bs-xpm-1994-05-11-1994131075-story.html.

Chapter Nine

George W. Bush (2001–2009) Administration

Background

George W. Bush, the son of George H.W. Bush, was sworn into office on was sworn into office on January 20, 2001, and left office on January 20, 2009. Bush's presidency was forced to respond to one of the most devastating incidents in American history on September 11, 2001, with the attack on the Twin Towers. Bush's presidency concentrated on the War on Terror, the No Child Left Behind Act, a response to Hurricane Katrina, issues related to stem cell research, and increasing upheaval over gay marriage and marriage equality. Interestingly, some of the OLC decisions relating to terrorism and the ramifications of a nation at war within its own bounds were never published directly.

Selected Memorandum Opinions under George W. Bush

Physician-Assisted Suicide

The OLC was asked to determine whether physician-assisted suicide serves a legitimate medical purpose under the Drug Enforcement Agency (DEA) regulations. The memorandum, somewhat longer than most issued by the OLC, was written by Sheldon Bradshaw and Robert Delahunty. Their conclusion was that there was no way to consider physician-assisted suicide to be a legitimate medical purpose, whether under state or federal laws. Further, they opined that even if a state decided to allow assisted suicide, the Controlled Substances Act at the Federal level would prohibit it.

Authority to Conduct Military Operations against Terrorists

In the days following the attack on the Twin Towers, President Bush turned to the OLC for legal counsel on dealing with the aftermath. On September 25, 2001, the OLC's John Yoo released his memorandum decision, which reported that:

> The President has broad constitutional power to take military action in response to the terrorist attacks on the United States on September 11, 2001. Congress has acknowledged this inherent executive power in both the War Powers Resolution and the Joint Resolution passed by Congress on September 14, 2001. (Yoo, 2001,188).

In a decision that would have far reaching implications, Yoo also found that the President had the power under the Constitution to retaliate against people, states, or organizations that might be suspected of being involved in terrorist attacks on the United States. He also suggested that the President had the right to retaliate against foreign states that were suspected of supporting terrorist organizations (Yoo, 2001). In doing so, the President had the right to release military forces "preemptively" against terrorist organizations, or the nations that support them. The most important clause in the memorandum may have been the ruling that the President had the right to do so, even if the organizations or states could not be tied to specific terrorist incidents related to the Twin Towers attack on September 2001 (Yoo, 2001).

In one of the longest of the OLC memos, Philbin (2001) provided a decision on the legality of the use of military commissions to try terrorists. Philbin was extremely thorough in his advice and provided a great deal of information to support the position that the President has the authority to establish military commissions that can be used to try, and then punish, terrorists that are linked to the 9/11 attacks. Philbin made a point to provide information used in support of the argument that the laws of armed conflict would apply in terrorist attacks. He stated that the President has the right to decide whether or not the nation has been attacked and is thus at war. Based on this contention, the 9/11 attacks could justifiably be considered war. However, under the laws established for war, the terrorists would be considered unlawful combatants. As such, they would be subject to being tried and punished for violating the laws of war. The President has the right to appoint military commissions to ensure this trial. As Philbin (2001, 238) stated, "...ample precedent establishes that military commissions may be used to try and punish (even with death) offenders under the laws of war." Philbin's decision, through the Office of Legal Counsel, was that "a declaration of war is not required to create a state of war or to subject persons to the laws of war, nor is it required that the United States be engaged in armed conflict with another nation" (2001, 239). This decision led the way for the entire handling of the war on terrorism, handling of prisoners at Gitmo, waterboarding, and the investigation later of John Yoo.

In a related question in 2002, Bybee (2002b) was asked to advise the President on the status of captured Taliban soldiers. The question was whether or not members of the Taliban militia would be entitled to protections as prisoners of war (POWs) under Article 4 of the Geneva Conventions of 1949. Bybee's conclusion was that the Taliban militia was not considered prisoners of war, because they did not meet three of the four established conditions for being lawful combatants. Further, Bybee found, there was no reason to arrange a formal tribunal in order to hold a hearing to determine status of any Taliban detainees.

Later in 2002, Bush asked the OLC to provide advice as to what authority the President had under both international and domestic law to use military force against the nation of Iraq. Bybee (2002a) pointed out in his response that this question had been addressed before; thus, he stated, this memo confirmed "prior advice" on the topic. Still, this was one of the OLC's longer memos and provided a very detailed document in support of the President's authority.

Summary of Additional Memorandum Opinions under George W. Bush

Within a month of the attack, Bush had asked the OLC's opinion as to whether or not it was legal to check names of people prohibited from purchasing firearms against the National Instant Criminal Background Check System, and if they could pass the results of the search along to the bureau of Alcohol, Traffic, and Firearms. The OLC's memorandum gave permission for the FBI to do so.

During the Bush Presidency, the Emoluments Clause also came under consideration. The Constitution has both a foreign and domestic Emoluments Clause, intended to prevent the President from losing his or her independence because of undue fiscal influences, both foreign and abroad. Although the technical definition of an emolument is an advantage received by holding office, the exact determination of what an emolument is can be hotly debated. The OLC has been asked to step in and provide advice upon more than one occasion. Koffsky (2001) issued an opinion that an international organization that the United States routinely participates in, such as the World Bank, is not a foreign state for purposes of the Emoluments Clause. Thus, employees of the Smithsonian (specifically mentioned in this case) would be able to participate by doing special projects under contract, without violating the Clause (Koffsky, 2001).

Within a month, Bush was asking the OLC to consider the recent United Nations Security Council Resolution regarding the President's authority to use military force against Iraq, based on international law. John Yoo (2002) authored the decision, which stated that the recent decision did not alter the legal authority that the UN Security Council had granted the US to use force against Iraq, based on the doctrine that the US could reasonably anticipate the need to do so in self-defense, or "anticipatory self-defense." The key would be if the President determined that the use of force would be necessary because of a threat that was imminent, and if the response was proportional in response to the threat that Iraq posed. Yoo (2002, 199) reiterated that the President had already been told that "the President has full constitutional authority as Chief Executive and Commander in Chief to use force against Iraq." Further, as Yoo stated, the US Congress had already given the President statutory authority to attack (2002).

Conclusions

Over the remainder of the Bush administration, the OLC's memorandum show a man who struggled mightily to help the nation recover from the 9/11 attacks, while improving America's education and dealing with ethical, moral, and legal considerations related to new technologies. In 2005, Hurricane Katrina hit and destroyed much of the South, leaving Bush to struggle with issues of thousands of homeless and jobless. By the time he left office in 2009, Bush had handled more major emergencies than any recent President.

References

"Opinions." (2020). *Justice.Gov.* https://www.justice.gov/olc/opinions?items_per_page=10&order=field_opinion_post_date&sort=asc&f%5B0%5D=field_opinion_post_date%3A1977.

Bradshaw, S., & Delahunty, R. (2001). Whether physician-assisted suicide serves a "legitimate medical purpose" under DEA regulations. *Justice.Gov.* https://www.justice.gov/file/19206/download.

Bybee, J. (2002a). Authority of the president under domestic and international law to use military force against Iraq. *Justice.Gov.* https://www.justice.gov/file/19036/download.

Bybee, J. (2002b). Status of Taliban forces under Article 4 of the Third Geneva Convention of 1949. *Justice.Gov.* https://www.justice.gov/file/19096/download.

Koffsky, D. (2001). Emoluments clause and world bank. *Justice.Gov.* https://www.justice.gov/file/19231/download.

Philbin, P. (2001). Legality of the use of military commissions to try terrorists. *Justice.Gov.* https://www.justice.gov/file/19121/download.

Yoo, J. (2001). The president's constitutional authority to conduct military operations against terrorists and nations supporting them. *Justice.Gov.* https://www.justice.gov/file/19151/download.

Yoo, J. (2002). Effect of a recent United Nations Security Council resolution on the authority of the President under International Law to use military force against Iraq. *Justice.Gov.* https://www.justice.gov/file/19031/download.

Chapter Ten

Barack Obama (2009–2017) Administration

Background

High levels of activity during the Obama administration led to extensive actions by the OLC. Chapter 10 focuses on the Affordable Care Act (also referred to as Obamacare), gay marriage and marriage equality, the War on Terror, and on a wide variety of foreign policy achievements. From the very beginning of his presidency, Obama sought to edit the structure that had been in place through OLC decision-making, resulting in the invalidation of a number of previous OLC decisions.

Selected Memorandum Opinions under Barak Obama

Memorandum Re-Considering Existing Decisions

The first decision under the Obama administration was whether or not the program EINSTEIN 2.0, which was to be installed in the unclassified offices of the Executive Branch, was written by Steven Bradbury

(Bradbury, 2009a). The question was whether or not the electronic security that was used to protect the Executive Office computer network violated the Fourth Amendment which prohibits unreasonable search and seizure. The allegation was made that the system violated the "Fourth Amendment to the Constitution, the Wiretap Act, the Foreign Intelligence Surveillance Act, the Stored Communications Act, and the pen register and trap and trace provisions of chapter 206 of title 18, United States Code" (Bradbury, 2009a, para. 1). Bradbury's conclusion was that the system required the permission of the user, which could be acquired by using long-on banners and an opt-in computer-user agreement that the technicians supporting the system would maintain. Thus, the system was authorized and did not violate any of the mentioned laws. By August, the President had asked that this decision be reviewed again; the decision was the same (Barron, 2009e).

The next issue addressed was whether or not an OLC memo from Lyndon Johnson's time authorizing polygraph usage under some circumstances was valid. Bradley concluded that the memo was not a formal decision and was no longer valid. Thus, the Oval Office was not bound by its authority to use polygraphs in the given circumstances (Bradbury, 2009b).

By early spring, the OLC was being asked to reconsider a wide variety of other decisions that had previously been issued. Four decisions relating to interrogations by the Central Intelligence Agency were authorized to be removed as they were considered no longer consistent with the views of the OLC (Barron, 2009a). No justification or explanation was given other than that the President had directed the decisions to be removed.

In short order, the OLC found that the Ronald Reagan Centennial Commission Act of 2009 was not in fact Constitutional and violated the "the Appointments Clause, the Ineligibility Clause, and the separation of powers" clauses (Lederman, 2009a). Following this decision, Barron (2009b) issued a memorandum reversing a 1987 opinion by the OLC that it was not legal to lower the salary of an appointee to make them eligible for a position that they would otherwise be eligible for.

In doing this, Barron essentially gave the executive office the ability to hire Senators or Representatives who would otherwise be ineligible. The next decision reversed a previous decision that found that using public money to meet with governments that support terrorism was unconstitutional (Barron, 2009c).

Barron (2009a) had previously, at the President's order, invalidated and withdrew four decisions relating to interrogation techniques used by the CIA. This Presidential order , was classified and had to be declassified to facilitate the release of the withdrawal. Ironically, Steven Bradbury, who was still a member of the OLC at the beginning of the Obama administration, was one of the authors of the original decision being reversed (Barron, 2009d).

As part of his campaign to have decisions reviewed, Obama asked to have the Constitutionality of the Matthew Shepard Hate Crimes Prevention Act reviewed, although a previous OLC decision had found the act Constitutional. The new decision was worded to ensure that the new President understood that this decision had already been made: "We therefore conclude, as we did in 2000," "As we explained in 2000," "Nothing in the law since 2000 calls this analysis into question," and "we adhere to our 2000 conclusion" (Lederman,2009b, 1–16).

In the last four months of 2009, the review continued, with the majority of the decisions supporting existing law. The one major exception was authored by Rhee (2009, 1) and concluded that the ten-year minimum sentence regarding "possession of a semiautomatic assault weapon in furtherance of a crime of violence or drug trafficking crime" was applicable. Rhee's decision was that "semiautomatic assault weapons are no longer among the firearms to which the ten-year minimum sentence" applied (2009, 1).

Decisions from the Second Year in Office: 2010

The frantic pace of the first year in office slowed in 2010, with most of the decisions addressing various "day to day" operations. One notable decision involved the DOJ views on a new Constitution proposed by the United States Virgin Islands. The decision by the DOJ/OLC regarding the proposed Constitution was that it would require a great deal of additional work to fit in with US law (Justice.gov, 2020). In other decisions, Applicability of tax levies of Thrift Savings Plan accounts were found to be valid and subject to IRS regulation. Applicability of various Emoluments were reviewed, as well as whether or not the Special Master for Troubled Asset Relief was required to be appointed by the President. In that case, it was acceptable for the Senate to make the decision (Justice.gov, 2020).

Four more important decisions were also produced. The first was that the Uniting and Strengthening America by Providing Appropriate Tools Required to Intercept and Obstruct Terrorism Act of 2001 did not require the Secretary of Commerce to give census information to law enforcement agencies, whether local or federal, if the information was prohibited from disclosure by the Census Act.

The next important decision was that the criminal provisions cited in the Violence Against Women Act would apply to conduct of woman-woman couples if it would be criminal if it were between a man and a woman. The OLC finding was that any violent action illegal between a man and a woman would also be illegal if it were between a woman and a woman. In another crime related decision, the OLC held that if the Crime Victims' Rights Act of 2004 applied to a case, the monies would be available to a victim from the time criminal proceedings were initiated, extending only to the time that the complaint was dismissed, whether it was dismissed by the victim or by the Government. Finally, in December the OLC found that if the Social Security Administration used Social Security Trust Funds to buy buildings and then sold them, the money did not need to go back into Social Security Trust. Instead, it would be acceptable for the GSA to put the money into the Federal Building Fund (Justice.gov, 2020). The OLC also determined that the President had the authority to use military force in Libya because it was in the national interest and also of short duration. Ackerman (2011) and Morrison (2011) both argued that this decision by the OLC undermines the traditional process of careful consideration and respect for the legal decisionmakers.

Summary of Additional Memorandum Opinions under Barack Obama

Other decisions issued by the OLC included the ruling that aliens admitted to the United States under a nonimmigrant visa cannot purchase guns in the US, but all other aliens must be allowed to purchase guns (Justice.gov, 2011, 2020). Interstate sales of lottery tickets were advised to be legal (Justice.gov, 2011, 2020). In 2012, one decision was issued that potentially impacts a great many people but is little known. The OLC held that neither citizens nor residents can be required to submit identifying data in order to view government websites (Justice.gov, 2012, 2020). The OLC also cautioned the President that for purpose of firearm sales, state of residency requirements were the same for both citizens and non-citizens. The OLC also held that the President could assert privilege if subpoenaed for the Fast and Furious investigation. Finally, in a potentially far-reaching decision, the OLC held that any professional on federal properties was bound to report suspected child abuse, regardless of where the child's home might be (Justice.gov, 2012, 2020).

The year 2013 saw no major decisions. In 2014, the decisions revolved around an increasing concern about terrorism. The OLC found that a prosecutor could decide to prosecute or not prosecute citations for contempt of Congress. The Assistant to the President and Director of the Office of Political Strategy and Outreach were found to be immune from subpoena. In late 2014, Homeland Security's authority to remove unlawfully present aliens was upheld, but Homeland Security was not allowed to defer removal of parents of DACA recipients. Finally, the OLC found that the President did have the authority to airstrike the Islamic State of Iraq and the Levant (Justice.gov, 2014, 2020).

In 2016, the last full year of Obama's Presidency, the Office of Legal Counsel was asked to advise the office of Management and Budget as to whether or not Congress could be banned from setting laws that would make the President keep quiet about legislation he felt was both necessary and expedient. They were also asked to issue a finding as to whether or not the President could be advised to keep quiet and fail to recommend *any* legislation. In specific, the question arose in conjunction with provisions for Medicare Modernization (Thompson, 2016).

The OLC found that the President has a duty to advise Congress and cannot be muzzled. Any provision requiring the President to act in any specific manner was regarded as advisory in nature and not binding ("Opinions," 2020).

Conclusions

During the Obama administration a number of groundbreaking changes occurred in the law, supported by the administration. The issues brought before the OLC, however, did not address many of the changes directly. Indeed, they seem to have skirted the major issues. One example was to question whether or not the Violence Against Women Act would be in effect for woman-on-woman domestic violence, clearly a lead into the marriage equality act masked in another issue.

References

"Opinions." (2020). *Justice.Gov.* https://www.justice.gov/olc/opinions?items_per_page=10&order=field_opinion_post_date&sort=asc&f%5B0%5D=field_opinion_post_date%3A1977.

Ackerman, B. (2011). Lost inside the Beltway. *Harvard Law Review 124*(7), 13–41.

Barron, D. (2009a). *Withdrawal of Office of Legal Counsel CIA interrogation options.* [online] Justice.gov. Available at: https://www.justice.gov/sites/default/files/olc/opinions/2009/04/31/withdrawalofficelegalcounsel_0.pdf [Accessed 17 May 2020].

Barron, D. (2009b). *Constitutionality of Section 7054 of the Fiscal Year 2009 Foreign Appropriations Act.* [online] Justice.gov. Available at: https://www.justice.gov/file/18496/download [Accessed 17 May 2020].

Barron, D. (2009c). *Validity of statutory rollbacks as a means of complying with the ineligibility clause.* [online] Justice.gov. Available at: https://www.justice.gov/file/18501/download [Accessed 31 May 2020].

Barron, D. (2009d). *Withdrawal of Office Of Legal Counsel Opinion.* [online] Justice.gov. Available at: https://www.justice.gov/file/18491/download [Accessed 19 May 2020].

Barron, D. (2009e). *Legality of intrusion-detection system to protect unclassified computer networks in the executive office.* [online] Justice.gov. Available at: https://www.justice.gov/file/18476/download [Accessed 17 May 2020].

Bradbury, S. (2009a). *Use of the EINSTEIN 2.0 Intrusion-Detection System to Protect Unclassified Computer Networks in the Executive Branch.* [online] Justice.gov. https://www.justice.gov/file/1346826/download.

Bradbury, S. (2009b). *Status of presidential memorandum addressing the use of polygraphs.* [online] Justice.org. Available at: https://www.justice.gov/file/18516/download [Accessed 15 May 2020].

Bradley, S. (2009). *Legal issues relating to the testing, use, and deployment of an intrusion-detection system (EINSTEIN 2.0) To protect unclassified computer networks in the executive branch.* [online] Justice.gov. Available at: https://www.justice.gov/olc/opinion/legal-issues-relating-testing-use-and-deployment-intrusion-detection-system-einstein-20 [Accessed 24 May 2020].

Justice.gov. 2011. (2020). *Opinions 2011.* [online] Available at: https://www.justice.gov/olc/opinions?f%5B0%5D=field_opinion_post_date%3A2011 [Accessed 13 May 2020].

Justice.gov. 2012. (2020). *Opinions* 2012 [online] Available at: https://www.justice.gov/olc/opinions?f%5B0%5D=field_opinion_post_date%3A2012 [Accessed 11 May 2020].

Justice.gov. 2014. (2020). *Opinions.* [online] Available at: https://www.justice.gov/olc/opinions?f%5B0%5D=field_opinion_post_date%3A2014 [Accessed 7 May 2020].

Justice.gov. (2020). *Opinions 2010.* [online] Available at: https://www.justice.gov/olc/opinions?f%5B0%5D=field_opinion_post_date%3A2010 [Accessed 12 May 2020].

Lederman, M. (2009a). *Constitutionality of the Ronald Reagan Centennial Commission Act Of 2009.* [online] Justice.gov. Available at: https://www.justice.gov/file/18506/download [Accessed 15 May 2020].

Lederman, M. (2009b). *Constitutionality of the Matthew Shepard hate Crimes Prevention Act.* [online] Justice.gov. Available at: https://www.justice.gov/file/18486/download [Accessed 17 May 2020].

Morrison, T. (2011). Constitutional Alarmism. *Harvard Law Review 124*(7), 1688–1749.

Rhee, J. (2009). *Whether the 10-year minimum sentence in 18 U.S.C. § 924(C)(1)(B)(I) applies to semi-automatic assault weapons.* [online] Justice.gov. Available at: https://www.justice.gov/file/18446/download [Accessed 18 May 2020].

Thompson, K. (2016). *Application of the recommendations clause to the Medicare Modernization Act.* [online] Justice.gov. Available at: https://www.justice.gov/opinion/file/929881/download [Accessed 9 May 2020].

Chapter Eleven

Donald Trump (2017–Present) Administration

Background

Chapter 11 focuses on executive orders produced early in Trump's administration, including opinions of the OLC relating to the travel ban relating to refugees, immigrants, non-immigrants, and green-card holders from specified Muslim-majority countries. Three travel bans were eventually issued, and the issue was addressed by the Supreme Court in September 2019. The importance of the OLC and its opinions relating to the future of America and America's immigration policy cannot be underestimated. This chapter is expected to be updated until this manuscript goes to press.

Selected Memorandum Opinions under Donald Trump

Early Decisions

The OLC was asked to determine whether or not the President John F. Kennedy Assassination Records Collection Act of 1992 allows a sitting

President to temporarily postpone the disclosure of historical but classified records if the content of the records is uncertain relative to national security. The question was whether or not the President had the right to hold back records or a portion of the records for closer examination, or whether they should be released automatically upon the release date. Gannon (2017) opined that "Serious constitutional concerns would arise if the Act were construed to require the President to make premature disclosures of records while they are likely to contain still-sensitive information" (Gannon, 2017, 1). Thus, the President was allowed to take more time to examine records that were scheduled to be released.

Throughout the history of the OLC, many of the questions revolved around the testimony of employees before various Congressional committees, or whether various persons could be forced to testify. In this case the OLC was requested to provide an opinion on whether an employee who was subpoenaed to appear before congressional committees and not allowed an agency counsel could have a private counsel, which would then be paid by the agency they worked for. Anders (2017) responded that in these circumstances the agency could hire and pay for a private attorney for the employee.

After this inauguration, Trump set out to establish his White House staff, with the result that White House Counsel asked for advice from the OLC on whether or not it would be nepotism to appoint his son-in-law to a position. Koffsky (2017) responded that the President had special privileges and thus it would not be nepotism to hire who he wanted for the position at issue. In a second major decision that first year, the OLC was asked to determine if it was acceptable for the Department of Defense to conduct background checks for its own employees and even determine whether or not these employees could see classified materials. It was Harris's (2018) opinion that this question had nothing to do with the president's role in security, and that it did not matter which branch conducted the investigation.

Travel Bans

In the early days of the Trump administration, President Trump issued an executive order banning travel into the United States from Iran,

Iraq, Libya, Somalia, Syria, Sudan, and Yemen for 120 days, and banning entry of refugees from Syria for an indefinite period (Varadarajan, 2019). Executive Order 13769, titled *Protecting the Nation from Foreign Terrorist Entry into the United States,* went into effect on January 27, 2017 (Gannon, 2020) and remained in effect until March 6, 2017, when it was superseded by Executive Order 13780, under the same title. The second Executive Order simply changed some of the provisions from the first order, provisions which had been successfully challenged in court.

There were several interesting considerations relating to the travel ban. The first is that the memorandum by the OLC associated with the travel ban was not released voluntarily to the public (Arnsdorf, 2017). The OLC simply used boiler plating or a template to describe what was in the executive order before signing off on the order (Arnsdorf, 2017). In order to get a copy of the memo, which was never published, the group POLITICO issued a Freedom of Information Request. The Justice Department, in response, released the Memorandum but stated that "this is generally the case under the Office's longstanding practice; however, it does not identify or contain substantive analysis of issues that were evaluated in the course of the review" (Arnsdorf, 2017, para. 4). The Acting Attorney General at the time, Sally Yates, stated that OLC reviews of executive orders had to be limited to whether or not the order appears to be lawful on its face, and whether or not it was properly drafted. No associated statements or issues could be considered (Arnsdorf, 2017). An executive order from 1962, issued by President John F. Kennedy, defined the process for preparing, presenting, filing, and publishing executive orders.

The Travel Ban and its subsequent iterations were one of the most controversial actions of a recent president and led to a number of court cases. The ban was even heard in the Supreme Court. The ban undoubtedly led to some of the other controversial actions reflected in later OLC decisions.

Additional Memorandum Opinions under Trump

In 2018 two more OLC decisions were issued that were controversial. The first related to airstrikes against Syrian chemical weapons facilities;

the second was regarding marijuana cultivation. In the first decision, Engel (2018) found that the President did have the lawful ability to direct airstrikes to take place on Syria's chemical weapons production facilities. The President had argued that the use of force was "in the national interest" and that he did not anticipate that the hostilities would extend to the level of war. Rather, the actions would be limited in scope. Based on these assertions, Engel found that the attacks were lawful. Interestingly, Engel states that "Prior to the Syrian operation, you requested our advice on the President's authority" (2018, 1) and that "we" [referring to the OLC] had given advice that the attack would be lawful. This suggests that there is an OLC memorandum at some point that has not been published or is classified, relating to this topic.

The Engel (2018) memorandum, perhaps more than most issued by the Office of Legal Counsel, provides a very in-depth review of the situation in Syria as of the time of production of the memo. It serves not only as a legal advice memorandum but will serve as a historical perspective for the future, as it documents thoroughly the situation in Syria. The memorandum addresses not only what targets were chosen and why, but also the powers of the Presidency that allowed the attacks. It also provides a great deal of case law and legislation relating to the President's authority to direct military actions from the beginning of the Republic.

The second controversial opinion appears to be a follow-on to the 1977 Ulman memo which discussed the growth of the giant scarlet poppy, the *Papaver bracteatum*. The memo, in response to a prompt by President Trump, appears to anticipate the relaxing of marijuana rules. Whitaker's memorandum opinion dated June 6, 2018, found that "the Drug Enforcement Administration may register an applicant to cultivate marijuana only if the registration scheme is consistent with the Single Convention on Narcotic Drugs," (2018, 1). The memorandum also reiterates that the Attorney General is authorized to license marijuana cultivation if he determines that it would be "consistent with the public interest and with United States obligations under international treaties, conventions, or protocols in effect on May 1, 1971" (Whitaker, 2018, 1). Whitaker points out that under the terms of the Single Convention of 1961, the nation must either completely stop marijuana production or limit it to oversight by a single government agency which will oversee growers and monopolize the wholesale marijuana trade. Whitaker concluded that as of the date of the memo, the United States was not meeting the requirement of the convention and the DEA needed to revise its procedures to comply. Whitaker (2018) pointed out that the concept of licensing the right to grow plants that can be used to process controlled substances is not a new one. Instead, there are a number of countries at present who license private growers of the opium poppy as well as coca bushes. Both of these plants are covered by the same treaty as cannabis sativa and hence set a precedent for processing under international law under the Single Convention. The President was advised that the DEA's rules need modification to comply with current international handling regulations as well as the Single Convention.

Summary of Additional Memorandum Opinions under Trump

Memorandums from 2019 and 2020 reflect an increasingly contentious environment surrounding President Trump. In 2019, the OLC addressed more than one question relating to the President's ability to designate acting directors of agencies. After several executions were postponed due to availability of the appropriate drugs, the OLC was asked to determine whether the Food and Drug Administration (FDA) even had jurisdiction over items used in lawful executions. The OLC response was that it did not.

In late May 2019, the OLC was asked to determine if the Former Counsel to the President could be given immunity for not testifying about his or her job. The OLC found that Congress cannot compel testimony, nor can a Former Counsel be penalized for following the President's request not to testify. The same immunity is granted to aides who decide not to testify to Congress ("Opinions 2019," 2020).

By June 2019, the OLC had been asked to advise on whether a Congressional request for the President's tax returns was legal. In this particular case the OLC reviewed all the associated materials and found that the request was a pretext, and stated that "under the facts and circumstances, the Secretary of the Treasury reasonably and correctly concluded that the Committee's asserted interest in reviewing the Internal Revenue Service's audits of presidential returns was pretextual and that its true aim was to make the President's tax returns public, which is not a legitimate legislative purpose" ("Opinions 2019," 2020). Thus, the request was denied. Had the request been for legitimate purpose it would likely not have been denied.

On July 9, 2020, the Supreme Court rejected President Trump's claims that he had immunity from both congressional investigation and law enforcement, a topic that had been the frequent subject of OLC decisions over the years. As this report detailed, whether or not sitting presidents could be indicted, what would be required for impeachment, and whether or not they had to comply with subpoenas had been a frequent question for the Office of Legal Counsel from a number of sitting presidents. The question seems to have been settled on July 9, 2020 when the Court rejected Trump's assertions that he did not have to comply with a subpoena from the Manhattan District Attorney to produce not only his personal financial records, but his business records. The decision was split, however, with the majority ruling that he did not have to release his records to Congress, at least not immediately (Barnes, 2020).

The Court put a hold on the subpoena from Congress, agreeing that Trump was trying to obfuscate Congress's ability to see his records while at the same time stating that Congress was deliberately overreaching in its requests. Both cases were returned to the lower courts, and Trump was told he could challenge the specific requests in that lower court (Barnes, 2020). He was given until July 27, 2020 to file the challenge, and on that date he did so, asking the Manhattan Court to declare the subpoenas invalid based on the belief that the intent was to harass, rather than to inform (Associated Press, 2020). The Manhattan court had asked for "detailed information about all of Trump's assets in the U.S. and abroad for a 10-year period," or, as Trump's lawyers stated, "it asks for everything" (Associated Press, 2020, para. 8–9). The subpoena covered a number of the states and entities in nine foreign countries.

The President's representatives referred to it as "an overreaching demand designed to pick apart the President" (Associated Press,

2020, para. 17). The legal team seemed to embrace the OLC's assertion that the request "was pretextual and that its true aim was to make the President's tax returns public, which is not a legitimate legislative purpose" ("Opinions 2019", 2020). Yet, the analysts' views of the ruling were split. Farivar (2020) argued that there are important ramifications from the decision. The first is that the Supreme Court made it clear that sitting presidents are *not* immune from criminal prosecution. This is in contradiction with prior interpretations of the law by the OLC.

The second important point is that the subpoena power of Congress is not without limits. During 2018 and 2019 four subpoenas had been issued by Congress in an effort to view the President's person tax returns and records. The Supreme Court ruled that Congress does have a right to investigate, but that the subpoenas as written violated the separation of powers principle and thus were not in the public interest. The Court commented that both Congress's legislative interests and the President's unique position were being violated. However, the Court did not prohibit subpoenaing the records, only that the scope of the subpoena needed to be no broader than "reasonably" necessary (Farivar, 2020). Congressional subpoenas will be required to give specific reasons for the subpoenas, not merely "for legislative purpose" or "for study for future legislation." This direction by the Court will undoubtedly enter case law to be used in future interpretation of presidential subpoenas.

Late in 2019, the OLC was asked to determine if someone who called in an "urgent concern" to the Inspector General would have their call forwarded to the intelligence communities. The OLC found that just because someone said they had an "urgent concern" did not mean the concern was actually urgent. Instead, if "the alleged conduct does not relate to 'the funding, administration, or operation of an intelligence activity" then it would not be considered urgent ("Opinions 2019," 2020).

In 2020, the OLC held that the Equal Rights Amendment could not be resuscitated based only on the desire to do so. Instead, expired potential amendments would be required to be re-started and re-voted in entirety ("Opinions 2020," 2020). The OLC also addressed questions related to the potential impeachment of the President, notably whether or not a committee for impeachment investigation had to authorized before it could begin work. In this particular case, several House committees issued subpoenas relating to the impeachment before there was ever a committee authorized to investigate impeachment. Thus, all of the subpoenas were pointless ("Opinions 2020," 2020).

Conclusions

From the very beginning of the Trump administration the nature of the questions directed to the OLC reflected the contentious nature of the administration itself. The majority of the questions that are publicly listed address either the appointment of temporary replacement organization heads, foreign policy problems, or issues related to Congressional appearance of individuals asked to testify against Presidential wishes.

References

"Opinions." (2020). *Justice.Gov.* https://www.justice.gov/olc/opinions?items_per_page=10&order=field_opinion_post_date&sort=asc&f%5B0%5D=field_opinion_post_date%3A1977.

"Opinions." (2020). *Justice.Gov.* https://www.justice.gov/olc/opinions?f%5B0%5D=field_opinion_post_date%3A2020.

"Opinions 2019." (2020). *Justice.Gov.* https://www.justice.gov/olc/opinions?f%5B0%5D=field_opinion_post_date%3A2019.

Anders, G. (2017). Authority of the Department of Health and Human Services to pay for private counsel to represent an employee before congressional committees. *Justice.Gov.* https://www.justice.gov/file/1078076/download.

Arnsdorf, I. (2017). Justice department releases letter approving travel ban. *Politico.* https://www.politico.com/story/2017/02/justice-department-trump-travel-ban-234561.

Associated Press. (2020). Trump lawyers challenge tax-records subpoena as 'harassment of the president'. *Marketwatch.* https://www.marketwatch.com/story/trump-lawyers-challenge-tax-records-subpoena-as-harassment-of-the-president-2020-07-27.

Barnes, R. (2020). Supreme Court says Manhattan prosecutor may pursue Trump's financial records, denies congress access for now. *Washington Post.* https://www.washingtonpost.com/politics/courts_law/supreme-court-trump-tax-returns-financial-records/2020/07/09/8f274352-c1e2-11ea-9fdd-b7ac6b051dc8_story.html.

Engel, S. (2018). April 2018 airstrikes against Syrian chemical-weapons facilities. *Justice.Gov.* https://www.justice.gov/olc/opinion/file/1067551/download.

Farivar, M. (2020). 3 key takeaways from US Supreme Court rulings on Trump's tax returns. *Voice of America*. https://www.voanews.com/usa/3-key-takeaways-us-supreme-court-rulings-trumps-tax-returns.

Gannon, C. (2017). Temporary Certification under the President John F. Kennedy Assassination Records Collection Act of 1992. *Justice.Gov*. https://www.justice.gov/olc/file/1078056/download.

Gannon, C. (2020). Re: proposed executive order entitled, "protecting the nation from foreign terrorist entry into the United States." *Politico.Com*. https://www.politico.com/f/?id=0000015a-00dd-deae-a75f-42fd5fd00002.

Harris, S. (2018). The Department of Defense's authority to conduct background investigations for its personnel. *Justice.Gov*. https://www.justice.gov/olc/file/1078041/download.

Koffsky, D. (2017). Application of the anti-nepotism statute to a presidential appointment in the white house office. *Justice.Gov*. https://www.justice.gov/olc/file/1085561/download.

Varadarajan, S. (2019). One year after the SCOTUS ruling: Understanding the muslim ban and how we'll keep fighting it—National Immigration Law Center. *National Immigration Law Center*. https://www.nilc.org/issues/immigration-enforcement/understanding-muslim-ban-one-year-after-ruling/.

Whitaker, H. (2018). Licensing marijuana cultivation in compliance with the single convention on narcotic drugs. *Justice.Gov*. https://www.justice.gov/olc/file/1272131/download.

Chapter Twelve

Discussion and Conclusions

Background

The OLC has generally performed its functions well and in a relatively politically non-involved manner throughout the years. The nature of the responses have evolved with the passing administrations. As the nation evolved, however, the clash between law and the federal government became more evident. In particular, it was the administration of George W. Bush that highlighted potential clashes of interest. In 2002, John Yoo of the OLC authored a memorandum that discussed the standards for conducting interrogations, commonly referred to in the media as the Bybee Memo (2002). This memo, written by Yoo but signed by Jay Bybee, the Assistant Attorney General, discussed what type of interrogation techniques (including waterboarding and other tortures) could legally be applied to terrorism suspects (Saltzman, 2010).

Four years later, the Office of Professional Responsibility (OPR) of the Department of Justice began investigating whether this memorandum, and others on the general topic, actually violated professional standards that the Justice Department expected its attorneys to adhere to (Saltzman, 2010). One of the issues was that it would have been impossible for Bush to have the power he did relating to the war on terrorism without the acquiescence of the OLC.

The investigation by the OPR determined that the memorandum in question violated ethical standards as well as the professional standards expected of OLC attorneys. The memorandums were essentially "torture memos" (Saltzman, 2010, 440). The OPR recommended that the attorneys who wrote the memos be disciplined. However, the Assistant Deputy Attorney General, David Margolis, provided a memo signed by the Attorney General, that dismissed the recommendation that the attorneys be referred to their state bar associations for discipline associated with ethical violations related to the memorandums. At issue, Margolis insisted, was that the OPR standard was higher than the one typically expected of attorneys. He argued that since the OLC attorneys had never been notified of the stricter standards, they could not be held accountable for upholding them. The other side of the argument, of course, is that neither Yoo nor Bybee upheld the standard generally expected of *any* government attorneys (Saltzman, 2010).

Part of the problem is that the nature of the OLC is in itself contradictory. The OLC is provide Presidents with advice and with opinions that they can accept. At the same time, they are expected to be independent of political pressures. Given that their advice is considered binding for the executive branch, this is a very difficult balancing act. In addition, the OLC serves as the attorney for the President and for the Attorney General. Saltzman (2010) argues that if the OLC uses a great deal of transparency, it will find the potential pressure from the White House and the Attorney General to be easier to stand up to, because there will be more support. Yet it can be very difficult to determine exactly what the OLC is doing and which products it is producing. It is one thing to have the OLC state that they produced a certain number of decisions during the year and quite another to find these decisions, even with the publishing of the Congressional Record and the OLC website. As noted in the research, it took a Freedom of Information Act request to find the memoranda associated with travel bans. This is despite the availability of the OLC "reading room" and lists of decisions (which, as this researcher experienced, are far from complete).

As long as the OLC has the ability to influence politics, it is critical that it avoid even the appearance of impropriety. The chief "take away" from the research thus far is that the set of activities assigned to the OLC may need to be split into two organizations, with legal advisors to the government and legal advisors to the President and Attorney General being separated.

Emoluments Clause

One of the questions that has arisen during the Trump presidency is the applicability of the Emoluments Clause. As of this writing, the OLC has not addressed the Emoluments Clause since 2010. It is important to remember that the OLC does not address issues unless someone from the executive branch asks them to (Blackman & Barrett, 2019). The Congressional Research Service[1]has weighed in on the matter but the OLC has, as of this writing, not been involved. As Chong (2020) has pointed out, any case that challenges the President's business dealings would be difficult for the government to win simply because it pits the Department of Justice against its own agency, the OLC. The OLC is arguably the most well-established authority on the Emoluments Clause. The OLC has released numerous recommendations on this topic, as discussed earlier in this book, meaning that for the Justice Department to proceed with any cases relating to emoluments against a President, the Department would be arguing against its own prior positions, a stance that will be both awkward and difficult to maintain.

Garrison (2012, 649) argues that the OLC is failing to fulfill its mandate and in fact, after 9/11, switched from a "Neutral Expositor of the best view of the law model and advanced a Private Lawyer model to advising the President." Chong (2020) would agree, arguing that the Department of Justice is avoiding contradicting itself many times by simply refusing to take more than a surface look at very difficult questions. Chong suggests that emoluments questions are actually quite simple: Is the President's pecuniary interest being served, or the public interest? This basic question does not warrant hundreds of pages of analysis when it could be answered in a simple paragraph in most cases. It is a subtle nod to the Garrison belief that the OLC is no longer fulfilling its mandates.

Deference to the OLC

Mittal (2015) argues that the position of the OLC has become diluted, most notably after the "war on terror" began in the Bush administration. In particular, she argues that when the OLC opinions relating to torture were leaked, and then withdrawn, the OLC showed that it was unlikely to be able to stand up to political pressure, in particular from the President's office. She argues that the OLC is in danger of becoming nothing but a "rubber stamp" of Presidents' opinions. She does point out that there are strong advocates for both sides of this argument, and that some analysts argue strongly that the OLC is fulfilling the mandate it was given to provide "best legal advice" relating to a President's questions and potential actions. It is undisputed that the OLC has the force of binding law within the executive branch. However, a more pertinent question may be what the role of the OLC is in other parts of the government and in the court systems. She questions how judges utilize OLC opinions, and whether or not they are required to respect and support them. If, for example, the OLC opinions are "entitled to judicial deference," what kind of deference would be given, and under what conditions? (Mittal, 2015, 212).

Some of the analysts believe that the OLC does indeed constrain Presidential power when constraint is needed. Others, however, insist that the OLC has departed from its mission. The OLC was developed to provide the executive branch with advice on what behaviors and decisions on a given topic would and would not be acceptable and within the bounds of law. However, in recent years, the OLC has issued decisions that are sometimes interpreted as having the bounds of law, when this is not the case. Instead, the Supreme Court has referred to various OLC decisions in a fashion that would suggest that the decisions are merely representations of historical perspectives or practices. This allows the Court to acknowledge what practices existed, and the law or decisions that supported the practices, without actually regarding the decisions as law. Mittal (2015) also suggests that when an agency consults the OLC, it can actually weaken their position if they end up going to court over the issue at some point, since agencies regarded as "expert agencies" will receive more deference from the courts than the OLC does. Thus, Mittal believes, agencies need to consider carefully whether or not they ask for a decision from the OLC. Once they receive a decision, it binds them; thus, it may be more efficacious to avoid asking for an OLC advice.

Modern Role of the OLC

Although the concentration of agencies must be to win in court, as illustrated in the previous section, suggesting that agencies should avoid seeking OLC advice, there is a corollary to this position. That corollary is that to a great extent, consulting with the Office of Legal Counsel has a certain level of immunity-conferring power. Attorney General Michael Mukasey testified in Congressional hearing that "the Justice Department… could not investigate or prosecute somebody for acting in reliance on a Justice Department opinion" regardless of whether or not that opinion proved to be incorrect (Harvard Law Review, 2008, 2086).

A *Note* by the Harvard Law Review supports the contention that the most obvious case of differences of opinion of the legal and moral "rightness" of a decision or series of OLC decisions might be related to torture and the war on terrorism, but the issues truly are not limited to this war. Instead, "It is potentially at stake every time the office interprets a criminal law that applies to the government" (Harvard Law Review, 2008, 2086).

The advisory functions of the OLC were originally developed in support of Article II of the Constitution which holds that it is the President's responsibility to ensure that the laws of the United States are "faithfully executed." (See U.S. CONST. art. II, § 3.) The President must understand enough law and its interpretation to know whether or not a law is legal before he can enforce it. Unless the President is an attorney before running for office, this can be exceptionally difficult to do if the President is functioning alone. It was for this reason that Congress gave the office of the Attorney General the obligation to assist and advise the President whenever he requested, or when any of the heads of Departments had questions.

When this process was instituted, the Assistant Solicitor General or Solicitor General provided the opinions in the Attorney General's name until the middle of the twentieth century. The Assistant Solicitor General's position was eliminated in 1950, and at this point the OLC took on the responsibility of writing the decisions. The Department of Justice regulations state that the OLC must give informal opinions to the Government agencies, as well as giving legal advice and assisting the Attorney General in their position as the President's legal advisory (Harvard Law Review, 2008). As this manuscript is being written, the OLC is the largest body in the United States that is tasked with interpreting the Constitution.

In private life, an individual who receives terrible or incompetent advice from their personal lawyer can sometimes mount a significant appeal based on the attorney's gross incompetence. The individual will not make much progress if he or she asserts that they conducted some act because their attorney told them it would be legal to do so. Instead, the process of justice occurs and in appeal they can assert that they received terrible advice. In an average person's life, criminals would have an argument that would nearly grant them immunity if the "bad lawyer" defense was used to excuse criminal behaviors at the beginning of the process. As the Harvard Law Review (2008) points out, when one is dealing with an issue that can affect the entire nation and the lawyer works for the government, the stakes are even higher; it is not just one life at stake. The government's attorneys have an obligation to get things right.

This puts a great deal of pressure on the OLC, which is being asked to make decisions that clarify law that even the leaders of the nation and the attorneys from other agencies are not able to understand. Further, the work the OLC does and the decisions they make originate, if not in the highest office of the land, in some of the highest offices. The pressure to "get things right" is immense, but part of the problem is that there is no real guidance in many cases for what is right. These are decisions that are by definition advice on new situations or situations in which the law is either conflicting or unclear. There are several very real concerns. While the idea that the decision could be a bad one and bring a great deal of pressure to the office (as in the case of Bush and Guantanamo), there is also an opportunity for the OLC attorneys to overreach and manipulate any particular situation. From a practical standpoint, it would stand to reason that the more high profile the decision is, the more political the decision is, and the more opportunity to pressure the OLC exists, the more likely it is that a decision could be bought or manipulated.

The OLC has a number of checks and balances in place to ensure that decisions do not go too far afield. They consider the OLC's culture, the pressures they are under, the need to minimize the number of times errors are made, the likelihood of self-serving decisions being presented, and whether the stances taken will be controversial. Bilder and Vagts (2008) asserted that the real problem may be determining what normal actually is. It is difficult to determine any absolute tests for a boundary for what is a "reasonable" legal argument; it is also difficult to determine what kind of test, if any, could be applied that would satisfy all constituents or stakeholders as to what would define a decision that would be considered completely unreasonable.

Part of this difficulty relates to the nature of the work and the importance of offering this legal advice at the highest levels of the government. Other difficulties, however, arise purely from American culture and from American's early definitions as a "melting pot." From the time the nation was established, a wide variety of cultures has been maintained from the original groups of citizens from multiple nations and creeds. It is difficult to foresee any single political or legal decision that would be accepted as being normal and moral by everyone. In fact, the opposite is true; it seems far more likely that no decision would meet these criteria. The next question that arises would be to ask how far afield, how far 'out there' a decision or position would have to be to be considered abnormal or immoral.

It was John Yoo's (2002) terror memos, and later his books, that may have brought this issue to a head (Yoo, 2007, 2008). Earlier, in Chapter Five (relating to Richard Nixon, the controversy over the secret taping of White House visitors, the break ins to Democratic headquarters, and the overall Watergate scandal) a number of divisive topics had been studied, ruled, and presented. It was, perhaps, a foreshadowing of what would later happen in the Bush White House. It would be difficult to argue that neither Nixon nor Bush acted incorrectly in consulting the OLC. The question arises, however, as to what types of pressure may have been put upon the OLC to provide answers that the sitting presidents would find acceptable. When Goldsmith (2009) took position in the OLC in 2003, he reported being so concerned over the way law had been interpreted that he wrote three different resignation letters, fearing his unpopular opinions about the OLC might get his position terminated.

One of the ways the OLC endeavors to remain in control of its own fate, and outside of the pressures that can exist in a highly charged political arena, is to require the individual agencies to seek help from their own General Counsels. The White House is the only Department or Agency that cannot be ignored or deterred. There are a variety of reasons for requiring the agencies to use their own Counsels; one of the strongest is simply to keep Agency employees from deliberately overworking the OLC with questions that may be frivolous. If the agencies or their agents were allowed to do this, it could slow the legal process in general, clog the OLC's office, and manipulate a situation in which agencies most in need might find real difficulty in getting their questions heard.

Another reason for requiring agencies to use their own General Counsels whenever possible is that it keeps the agencies from deliberately asking for decisions on serious but contentious matters so that the OLC would be under pressure to produce a decision rather than the agency itself. As the political arena in the United States becomes increasingly contentious, it is understandable that individual agencies or departments, and even their General Counsels, would seek to be kept at arms' length from controversial questions and what might be painful decisions. The OLC does reserve the right to accept issues from agencies if the there is a justifiable reason that the decision should be made from the OLC's office and not at a departmental level.

Ackerman (2010) was so concerned that the OLC was becoming politicized that he proposed setting up a nine-judge panel to represent the Executive Branch, but not necessarily the President. These judges would have four-year terms, and the terms would be staggered. Thus, each sitting President would be able to nominate three judges during each term. The Senate would have to confirm the judges, in order to pressure the President to nominate strong and reputable jurists who were not prone to acting like political party members. In this way, Ackerman (2010) asserted that the judges would look like a court and act like a court, rather than being there in support of the power of the president. Such a tribunal would be able to stop unilateral assertions of authority which Ackerman clearly believes the OLC has surrendered to. Ironically, Ackerman believes that the final decision on whether or not a situation is legal or constitutional would then be made by the President, and the President could ignore advisory opinions produced by the OLC judicial panel. He concedes his idea is not perfect, but it would support the Founding Fathers' intent to have separation of powers. Unfortunately, if Ackerman's plan came to fruition, it would likely be seen by the courts as contradictory to the very separation of powers that the plan aims to protect.

At the present time, the OLC declines to write decisions on matters that are already being litigated. It would be extremely divisive to consent to provide a decision on a matter that is already being litigated or is pending hearing before the Supreme Court. It could also set up a situation where the OLC would be providing decisions that could be in direct contrast with the Department of Justice's active cases. The stress that this could put on the justice system as a whole has the potential to be tremendously expensive and even destabilizing for the citizens who are awaiting decisions. It would be extremely difficult to explain that the Justice Department as a whole believed that the position on an issue should be one thing (and to have law to support it) while a division of Justice, the OLC, argued the exact opposite – and also had law to support it.

One of the reasons that the OLC has formalized the process is so that all of the decisions are carefully researched ; the idea of off-the-cuff legal advice on a matter of national importance is simply staggering. Providing various organizations and the President's office with, for example, an oral response to their questions rather than providing a well-reasoned and legally supported document, tracked and signed, would be extremely impractical and allows for accusations of "he said, she said" which would inevitably result from a more informal process. The Harvard Law Review (2008, 2090) makes another point: "The formality also helps prevent recipients from exaggerating or selectively comprehending nuanced analyses," which would only serve to obfuscate rather than clarify the issues.

Some of the OLC's decisions are classified; other decisions are not published because of their content even though they are not technically classified. In addition, many of the opinions are not made available to the public until some years after the decisions have been rendered and presented to the President or the agency that requested them. According to the Harvard Law Review (2008) the reason for delaying publishing decisions or to decline to make them public is that the decision has to be able to hold up under public scrutiny. If there is classified information in the decision, or information that it would be safer or better for the public to not know, then it is reasonable that the publishing of the decision be withheld or postponed (Harvard Law Review, 2008). Goitein (2016) disagrees, however; she believes that the government is relying on what she refers to as "secret law" when they are not open and transparent. As she pointed out, "What qualifies as 'law' — and, for that matter, how 'secret' the law must be in order to raise concerns — are threshold questions that have received little attention" (Goitein, 2016, 2). The core of her argument appears to be that if the people are not allowed a great deal of transparency, they will not be informed, and without being informed they will not be able to understand what the legislature intended, and why it is necessary. More importantly, when they do not know what the law is, they cannot discuss it with their representatives and urge them to a particular cause of action (Goitein, 2016).

One of the keenest issues relating to the use of OLC decisions as a basis for deciding justice or guiding one's behavior is the consideration of qualified immunity. While qualified immunity as a concept was probably developed to ensure that a public servant, in the commission of their work, could not be sued if they deviated from the norm somewhat and made a relatively insignificant error, qualified immunity actually ensure that there is an allowed margin of error before an official or governmental employee can be sued (Harvard Law Review, 2008).

In a civil case there is a wide swath which would have to be violated before qualified immunity did not protect the practitioner. Officials would not be held responsible if "their conduct does not violate clearly established statutory or constitutional rights of which a reasonable person would have known," (*Harlow v. Fitzgerald*, 1982, 457). In essence, qualified immunity protects anyone who is not blatantly incompetent. The concept of the "reasonable person," so prevalent in law corners, is utilized in the determination of whether or not an official should receive qualified immunity. Absent deliberate and malicious intent, it is likely that the individual would be protected by the law regardless of the right- or wrong- ness of the OLC's advice. The case of *Harlow v. Fitzgerald* (1982) came to prominence after an individual filed suit because he believed he was fired by the Department of the Air Force, along with White House aides to former President Nixon, in retaliation for their actions in working for Nixon. The primary holding differed with OLC opinions of the time and stated that "Qualified immunity applies to presidential aides regarding their official actions, and it can be penetrated only when they have violated clearly established statutory or constitutional rights" (*Harlow v. Fitzgerald*, 457 U.S. 800 (1982), Primary Holding).

Ackerman (2010, 3) may be somewhat of an alarmist; he asserts that something is seriously wrong with the American system of government; he swears that the presidency has evolved into "an especially dangerous office" which actually threatens the Constitution (Ackerman, 2010, 4). He urges Americans to "act before it is too late," (Ackerman, 2010, 11). However, as Morrison (2011, 1688) points out, this type of concern is not new; Ackerman simply writes in the tradition of more urgent convictions.

Ackerman (2010) and Morrison (2011) agree on a few things and disagree on many. They both agree, for example, that tacitly pressuring the OLC to produce a legal recommendation that would allow President Bush to personally approve waterboarding was worse than Nixon's decision to just do what he wanted in terms of Watergate (Ackerman, 2011). Morrison, however, believes that Bush's actions and those of the OLC represented what was essentially an accident resulting from a "combination of political, ideological, and psychological factors to which no structure could ever be entirely immune" (Morrison, 2011, 1743).

Throughout this chapter, suggestions by various analysts have been presented. It was Cover (2012) that suggested that one of the main problems is the need for ethical reform in the OLC. By having a broad base of qualified immunity, there was little ability to hold supervisors responsible for the actions or decisions of those attorneys writing the memos. Indeed, one might ask why anyone would bother if there can be no action against the OLC as a whole. However, Cover argues that if there is no way to hold lawyers accountable for their ethical failures or the failures of their subordinates, there is no point in exploring proposals that have the goal to protect the OLC. Even if qualified immunity were stripped from the OLC, or limited to a great extent, other steps would need to be taken. Ackerman (2010) suggested increasing the number of attorneys and utilizing a panel of jurists to produce the decisions. Cover (2012) also suggests using a larger number of senior lawyers, who would review proposed OLC decisions and then either sign off on them or require that deficiencies be corrected before being signed. This simple procedure change, it is suggested, would increase OLC oversight, improve accountability, and result in legal advice that is both better and more independent.

Garrison (2013) suggests that it is very imperative to understand how the Office of the Attorney General, and subsequently the OLC, operates because of how important the power to give legal opinions within the executive branch is. One of the biggest problems in understanding what occurred and how it occurred, he suggests, is that there has not been a development of adequate literature regarding the evolution of ethical boundaries. The Attorney General's office was originally a part time position with no "perks," not even a staff or office supplies.

George Washington appears to have had great difficulty finding an Attorney who would serve as Attorney General, the conditions were so bad. In fact, Washington lured Edmund Randolph, the candidate, by telling him it would be easier to attract clients if he took the position (Garrison, 2013). Garrison reports that William Barr, when he discovered what Washington offered Randolph, said "so much for government ethics in those days" (Garrison, 2013, 222).

Levity aside, both Garrison and Barr have a point: government ethics have generally been a bit lacking. Indeed, this suggests one of the reasons that the Office of Legal Counsel has been so important. It is the only office regularly available to the White House to gather what is expected to be dispassionate and disconnected analysis of the law, without regard to what the White House may, or may not like. Yet in conducting the research for this book, it became clear that it would be impossible for the OLC to fail to determine what the President's wishes were. The very nature of the questions that the Presidents over the years have asked the OLC to rule on would serve to alert the OLC to the answers the President wanted. Thus, the OLC had two possible responses: produce an answer that would support the President's actions, and thus provide them with perceived legitimacy, or provide an answer that would frustrate, and perhaps anger, the President, and potentially place the office at risk. The research showed that when possible, the OLC provided responses that would placate or support the President. When they could not, the responses were not published or perhaps were redacted or made into classified documents. While this did not happen all the time, it happened enough that Garrison, Ackerman, Morrison, and other analysts have concluded that it is past time for revisions to the operation of the office.

Conclusions

One thread that evolved throughout the course of the book was OLC advice relating to impeachment, beginning with President Richard M. Nixon, reaching through impeachment actions of President William Clinton, and now multiple impeachments of President Trump. The OLC was kept busy providing legal opinions into investigation of Trump's actions, actions of the FBI, and legal issues relating to potential impeachment actions. It is likely that the OLC will end up working extra hours to accommodate questions relating to what a highly contested election 2020 was.

Several possible reforms were discussed in this chapter and the author wanted to provide them initially in an impartial way without providing a personal opinion about whether such reforms would be beneficial or not. This conclusion section is the best place for such an analysis. The author can certainly defend the notion to split the functions of the OLC into two separate divisions so that the President receives advice on constitutional issues from one division and the rest of the executive branch receives advice from another division. It would certainly bring the appearance of independence and impartiality to the division not tied directly to the President. The problem is the practical reality would seem to make the arrangement either unworkable or not have the desired effects. The President already has a set of personal advisers in the Executive Office of the President and the internal tension between the President and the Justice Department or OLC continues to exist. The President would also be able to apply indirect political pressure on the second division through leadership appointments or other processes. More accountability in government is always welcome but the argument can be made that the people who would be held responsible for mistakes either become known (Yoo and Bybee for example) or hold positions that would lead to dismissals or resignations (Attorney General, Assistant Attorney General, etc.). During the course of research and writing this book, it was even challenging to find out the names of the rank-and-file attorneys of the OLC so requiring more signatures on opinions from staff would be wonderful for the purpose of transparency or simply provide the benefit of having more information available. Of course, the Department of Justice (2010) memorandum on best practices for OLC written opinions indicates that the existing process strives for the highest level of quality and professionalism. If the process is followed as written, the only question would be if any mistake made is intentional (and likely worthy of sanctions) or unavoidable.

As noted in Chapter 1, OLC opinions tend to overwhelmingly support the legal position taken by the President. Cover (2012) notes that 79% percent of OLC opinions fully support the President and an additional 8% of opinions partially support the President in the timeframe covering the Carter administration to the first year of the Obama administration. From a personal point of view, it is hard to say whether that reality is problematic or not. It is almost certain that the President makes their position clear to the OLC when asking for an opinion by how they frame their question or through direct communication. Lawyers are also ethically bound to zealously defend their client and, as much as the client is expected to be the American people, it is more candid to believe that the OLC represents the only one nationally elected by the public as their chosen leader – the President. After reading many OLC opinions, it is also clear that OLC attorneys objectively advise the President by looking at historical precedents and trying to look at both sides of an issue. This author would argue that the best reform is simply more transparency by requiring many more OLC opinions to be released to the public after an appropriate number of years of passed to alleviate any national security or other concerns. The only disappointments of writing this book were the inability of finding any former OLC attorney willing to discuss their years of service on record and only having access to roughly 25 percent of existing OLC opinions. To be clear, it is completely understandable why these attorneys did not want to speak on record and their commitment to professional ethics should be applauded. Qualified immunity is also very worthwhile to keep in place for these highly trained lawyers.

On a final note, as of January 2021, it is important to consider future activities under a Biden administration and make a final appraisal of OLC activities under President Trump. Like several presidents before him, President Trump expected loyalty from the Justice Department and the OLC. President Trump has the perception, if not the reality, of being more willing to release favorable OLC opinions after taking a position publicly than at least some of his predecessors. These actions were clearly an effort to add legitimacy to his position for better or worse. The Trump administration is certainly more transparent in terms of releasing OLC opinions than several previous presidencies. It is too early to tell exactly how the OLC would function under President Biden because there are simply too many variables at this point in time. The most obvious variables include what decisions potential Attorney General Merrick Garland or the Assistant Attorney General in charge of the OLC decide to take . Based on the cabinet choices that have been announced, the Obama administration should be considered an excellent blueprint. It will also be interesting to see how Biden navigates a polarized country after a contested election, an internal battle within his own Democratic party between the moderates and progressives that no longer has the common enemy of President Trump, as well as the pandemic of course.

Note

1 See *The Emoluments Clauses of the US Constitution* (2020), at https://fas.org/sgp/crs/misc/IF11086.pdf.

References

Ackerman, B. (2010). *The decline and fall of the American Republic.* Cambridge: Harvard University Press. (Book discusses OLC and calls for reform – leads to written debate between Professors Ackerman and Morrison in Harvard Law Review)

Bilder, R. B., & Vagts, D. F. (2008). Speaking law to power: Lawyers and torture. *American Journal of International Law, 98*(2004), 689. https://heinonline.org/HOL/LandingPage? handle=hein.journals/ajil98&div=64&id=&page=.

Blackman, J., & Tillman, S. B. (2019). The office of legal counsel has not shifted its position on whether the foreign emoluments clause applies to the president. But the civil division has. *Reason.Com.* https://reason.com/2019/10/04/ the-office-of-legal-counsel-has-not-shifted-its-position-on-whether-the-foreign-emoluments-clause-applies-to-the-president-but-the-civil-division-has/.

Bybee, J. (2002).Memorandum for Alberto R. Gonzales counsel to the president, [online] Department of Justice. Available at https://nsarchive2.gwu.edu/NSAEBB/NSAEBB127/02.08.01.pdf.

Chong, J. (2020). The Justice Department has had to twist itself in knots to defend Trump on emoluments. *The Atlantic.* https://www.theatlantic.com/ideas/archive/2020/05/dojs-about-face-emoluments/612004/.

Cover, A. (2012). Supervisory responsibility for the office of legal counsel. *The Georgetown Journal of Legal Ethics, 25,* 269–315. https://scholarlycommons.law.case.edu/cgi/viewcontent.cgi?article=1597&context=faculty_publications.

Department of Justice. (2018). Office of Legal Counsel: Best practices for OLC Legal advice and written opinions. Last modified July 16, 2014. https://www.justice.gov/olc/best-practices-olc-legal-advice-and-written-opinions.

Garrison, A. (2012). The opinions by the Attorney General and the Office of Legal Counsel: How and why they are significant. *Albany Law Review, 76*(1), 217–245.

Garrison, A. (2013). The opinions by the Attorney General and the Office of Legal Counsel: How and why they are significant. *Albany Law Review, 76*(1), 217–245.

Goitein, Elizabeth and the Brennan Center for Justice. (2016). The new era of secret law. Accessed March 15, 2018. https://www.brennancenter.org/sites/default/files/publications/The_New_Era_of_Secret_Law.pdf.

Goldsmith, J. (2009). *The terror presidency: Law and judgement inside the Bush Administration*. New York: W.W. Norton and Company.

Harlow v. Fitzgerald, 457 U.S. 800 (1982).

Harvard Law Review. (2008). Note: The immunity-conferring power of the Office of Legal Counsel. 2008. *Harvard Law Review, 121*(8), 2086–2109.

Mittal, S. (2015). OLC's day in court: Judicial deference to the Office of Legal Counsel." *Harvard Law and Policy Review, 9*(1), 211–240.

Morrison, T. (2011). Constitutional alarmism. *Harvard Law Review, 124*(7), 1688–1749. (Book Review of Ackerman book listed above)

Saltzman, R. (2010). Executive power and the Office Of Legal Counsel. *Yale Law & Policy Review*. https://digitalcommons.law.yale.edu/cgi/viewcontent.cgi?article=1598&context=ylpr.

Yoo, J. (2002).Memorandum for Alberto R. Gonzales counsel to the president. [online] *Department of Justice*. Available at https://nsarchive2.gwu.edu/NSAEBB/NSAEBB127/02.08.01.pdf.

Yoo, J. (2007). *War by other means*. New York: Grove/Atlantic, Inc.

Yoo, J. (2008). *The powers of war and peace: the constitution and foreign affairs after 9/11*. Chicago, IL: University of Chicago Press

References

"25th Amendment." (2019). *History*. https://www.history.com/topics/united-states-constitution/25th-amendment.

"Article 1 Section 3 Clause 7 Constitution." (2020). *Constitution.Congress.Gov*. https://constitution.congress.gov/browse/article-1/section-3/clause-7/.

"Executive orders disposition tables index.". (2019). *National Archives*. https://www.archives.gov/federal-register/executive-orders/disposition.

"Jimmy Carter quick facts." (2020). *Jimmy Carter*. https://jimmycarter.info/president-mrs-carter/jimmy-carter-quick-facts-bio/.

"Libguides: Gray literature 101: Introduction." (2019). *Libguides.Health.Unm.Edu*. https://libguides.health.unm.edu/graylit.

"Libguides: Systematic reviews: Conducting, finding and appraising: Searching the gray literature." (2019). *Guides.Library.Cmu.Edu*. https://guides.library.cmu.edu/c.php?g=586398&p=4050795.

"Office of Legal Counsel." (2016). *Allgov.Com*. http://www.allgov.com/departments/department-of-justice/office-of-legal-counsel?agencyid=7437.

"Opinions." (2020). *Justice.Gov*. https://www.justice.gov/olc/opinions?f%5B0%5D=-field_opinion_post_date%3A1981&f%5B1%5D=field_opinion_post_date%3A1981-04.

"Opinions 1961." (2019). *Justice.Gov*. https://www.justice.gov/olc/opinions?f%5B0%5D=field_opinion_post_date%3A1961.

"Opinions 1976." (2020). *Justice.Gov*. https://www.justice.gov/olc/opinions?f%5B0%5D=field_opinion_post_date%3A1976.

"Opinions 1977." (2020). *Justice.Gov.* https://www.justice.gov/olc/opinions?items_per_page=10&order=field_opinion_post_date&sort=asc&f%5B0%5D=field_opinion_post_date%3A1977.

"Opinions 2019." (2020). *Justice.Gov.* https://www.justice.gov/olc/opinions?f%5B0%5D=field_opinion_post_date%3A2019.

"Opinions 2020." (2020). *Justice.Gov.* https://www.justice.gov/olc/opinions?f%5B0%5D=field_opinion_post_date%3A2020.

"Organization, mission and functions manual." (2012). *Justice.Gov.* https://www.justice.gov/jmd/organization-mission-and-functions-manual.

"Organization, mission & functions manual: Attorney General, Deputy and Associate." (2014). *Justice.Gov.* https://www.justice.gov/jmd/organization-mission-and-functions-manual-attorney-general#ag.

"Organization, mission and functions manual: Office of Legal Counsel." (2014). *Justice.Gov.* https://www.justice.gov/jmd/organization-mission-and-functions-manual-office-legal-counsel.

"President Clinton's impeachment trial begins." (2020). *History.* https://www.history.com/this-day-in-history/clinton-impeachment-trial-begins.

"Richard Nixon—Key events." (2019). *Miller Center.* https://millercenter.org/president/richard-nixon/key-events.

"Richard Nixon (1913–1994)." (2019). *Biography.Com.* https://www.biography.com/us-president/richard-nixon.

"Truman executive orders disposition tables." (2019). *National Archives.* https://www.archives.gov/federal-register/executive-orders/truman.html.

31 U.S.C. § 11(d) (1950).

Arnsdorf, I. (2017). Justice department releases letter approving travel ban. *Politico.* https://www.politico.com/story/2017/02/justice-department-trump-travel-ban-234561.

Associated Press. (2020). Trump lawyers challenge tax-records subpoena as "harassment of the president". *Marketwatch.* https://www.marketwatch.com/story/trump-lawyers-challenge-tax-records-subpoena-as-harassment-of-the-president-2020-07-27.

Barnes, R. (2020). Supreme court says Manhattan prosecutor may pursue Trump's financial records, denies congress access for now. *Washington Post.* https://www.washingtonpost.com/politics/courts_law/supreme-court-trump-tax-returns-financial-records/2020/07/09/8f274352-c1e2-11ea-9fdd-b7ac6b051dc8_story.html.

Barr, W. (1989a). Authority of the customs service to offer rewards for information concerning the whereabouts of indicted drug traffickers. *Justice.Gov.* https://www.justice.gov/file/24231/download.

Barr, W. (1989b). Authority of the Federal Bureau of Investigation to override International Law in Extraterritorial Law Enforcement activities. *Justice.Gov.* https://www.justice.gov/file/24241/download.

Barron, D. (2009a). *Withdrawal of office of legal counsel CIA interrogation options.* [online] Justice.gov. Available at: https://www.justice.gov/sites/default/files/olc/opinions/2009/04/31/withdrawalofficelegalcounsel_0.pdf [Accessed 17 May 2020].

Barron, D. (2009b). *Constitutionality of Section 7054 of the Fiscal Year 2009 Foreign Appropriations Act*. [online] Justice.gov. Available at: https://www.justice.gov/file/18496/download [Accessed 17 May 2020].

Barron, D. (2009c). *Validity of statutory rollbacks as a means of complying with the ineligibility clause*. [online] Justice.gov. Available at: https://www.justice.gov/file/18501/download [Accessed 31 May 2020].

Barron, D. (2009d.). *Withdrawal of office of legal counsel opinion*. [online] Justice.gov. Available at: https://www.justice.gov/file/18491/download [Accessed 19 May 2020].

Barron, D. (2009e). *Legality of intrusion-detection system to protect unclassified computer networks in the executive office*. [online] Justice.gov. Available at: https://www.justice.gov/file/18476/download [Accessed 17 May 2020].

Bell, G. (1936). Filling the vacancy following the death of the secretary of war. *Justice Department*. https://www.justice.gov/file/20651/download.

Bell, G. (1937a). Censorship of transmission of Trotzky speech from Mexico. *Justice Department*. https://www.justice.gov/file/20656/download.

Bell, G. (1937b). The president's power in the field of foreign relations. *Justice Department*. https://www.justice.gov/file/20661/download.

Bell, G. (1939a). Jurisdiction and procedure of the office of the Assistant Solicitor General. *Department of Justice*. https://www.justice.gov/file/19196/download.

Bell, G. (1939b). Presidential authority to order the removal of the original engrossed constitution from the library of congress. *Department of Justice*. https://www.justice.gov/file/20671/download.

Bilder, R.B., & Vagts, D. F. (2008). Speaking law to power: Lawyers and torture. *American Journal of International Law, 98*(2004), 689. https://heinonline.org/HOL/LandingPage?handle=hein.journals/ajil98&div=64&id=&page=.

Black, J. (2018). Eisenhower and the cold war. *Foreign Policy Research Institute*. https://www.fpri.org/article/2018/02/eisenhower-cold-war/.

Blackman, J., & Tillman, S. B. (2019). The office of legal counsel has not shifted its position on whether the foreign emoluments clause applies to the president, but the civil division has. *Reason.Com*. https://reason.com/2019/10/04/ the-office-of-legal-counsel-has-not-shifted-its-position-on-whether-the-foreign-emoluments-clause-applies-to-the-president-but-the-civil-division-has/.

Bradbury, S. (2009b). *Status of Presidential Memorandum addressing the use of polygraphs*. [online] Justice.org. Available at: https://www.justice.gov/file/18516/download [Accessed 15 May 2020].

Bradley, S. (2009). *Legal issues relating to the testing, use, and deployment of an intrusion-detection system (EINSTEIN 2.0) To protect unclassified computer networks in the executive branch*. [online] Justice.gov. Available at: https://www.justice.gov/olc/opinion/legal-issues-relating-testing-use-and-deployment-intrusion-detection-system-einstein-20 [Accessed 24 May 2020].

Bradshaw, S., & Delahunty, R. (2001). Whether physician-assisted suicide serves a "legitimate medical purpose" under DEA Regulations. *Justice.Gov*. https://www.justice.gov/file/19206/download.

Brown *v. Board of Education*, 347 U.S. 483 (1954).
Brown *v. Board of Education II*, 349 US 294 (1955).
Bybee, J. (2002a). Authority of the president under domestic and international law to use military force against Iraq. *Justice.Gov.* https://www.justice.gov/file/19036/download.
Bybee, J. (2002b). Status of Taliban forces under Article 4 of the Third Geneva Convention of 1949. *Justice.Gov.* https://www.justice.gov/file/19096/download.
Carey, H. F. (1997). The UN humanitarian intervention in Haiti and the development of a human rights enforcement regime. *Journal of Haitian Studies, 3/4*, 30–47.
Chong, J. (2020). The Justice Department has had to twist itself in knots to defend Trump on emoluments. *The Atlantic.* https://www.theatlantic.com/ideas/archive/2020/05/dojs-about-face-emoluments/612004/.
Clark, T. (1946). Presidential appointment of Justice Robert Jackson to prosecute axis war criminals in Europe. *Justice Department.* https://www.justice.gov/file/20621/download.
Clintonv. Jones, 520 U.S. 681 (1997) https://supreme.justia.com/cases/federal/us/520/681/.
Cover, A. (2012). Supervisory Responsibility for the office of legal counsel. *The Georgetown Journal of Legal Ethics, 25*, 269–315. https://scholarlycommons.law.case.edu/cgi/ viewcontent.cgi?article=1597&context=faculty_publications.
Cox, O. (1942a). Criminal liability for newspaper publication of naval secrets. *Justice Department.* https://www.justice.gov/file/20691/download.
Cox, O. (1942b). Removal of Japanese aliens and citizens from Hawaii to the United States. *Justice Department.* https://www.justice.gov/file/20681/download.
Cox, O. (1942c). Trials of newspaper personnel accused of disclosing naval secrets. *Justice Department.* https://www.justice.gov/file/20696/download.
Crabtree, B., & Miller, W. (Eds.). (1999). *Doing qualitative research.* Thousand Oaks, CA: Sage.
Cummings, H. (1934). Legality of an executive order requiring executive departments and independent establishments to make monthly financial reports. *Justice.Gov.* https://www.justice.gov/file/19181/download.
D'Amato, D. (2017). The gold clause cases. *The Future of Freedom Foundation.* https://www.fff.org/explore-freedom/article/gold-clause-cases/.
Dellinger, W. (1994). Deployment of United States armed forces into Haiti. *Justice.Gov.* https://www.justice.gov/file/20306/download.
Dellinger, W. (1995). The balanced budget amendment. *Justice.Gov.* https://www.justice.gov/file/20261/download.
Dellinger, W., & Powell, H. J. (1993). Constitutionality of health care reform. *Justice.Gov.* https://www.justice.gov/file/20451/download.
Department of Justice. (2018a). Office of Legal Counsel. Last modified November 28, 2017. https://www.justice.gov/olc. (Discussed earlier in Proposal)
Department of Justice. (2018b). Office of Legal Counsel: Best practices for OLC legal advice and written opinions. Last modified July 16, 2014. https://www.justice.gov/olc/best-practices-olc-legal-advice-and-written-opinions. (Discussed earlier in Proposal)

Department of Justice. (2018c). Office of Legal Counsel: FOIA electronic reading room. Last modified November 8, 2017. https://www.justice.gov/olc/olc-foia-electronic-reading-room. (Discussed earlier in Proposal)

Department of Justice. (2018d). Office of Legal Counsel: Opinions. Last modified June 5, 2016. https://www.justice.gov/olc/opinions-main. (Discussed earlier in Proposal)

Dixon, R. G. (1973). Amenability of the president, vice president and other civil officers to federal criminal prosecution while in office. *Department of Justice*. https://fas.org/irp/agency/doj/olc/092473.pdf.

Eberly, W. (1943). Presidential appointment of foreign agents without the consent of the senate. *Justice Department*. https://www.justice.gov/file/20891/download.

Eberly, W. (1945). Implementation Of International Civil Aviation Agreements. *Justice Department*. https://www.justice.gov/file/20701/download.

Eiteljorg, H. (2008). Grey literature: An obvious candidate for online access. *CSA Network*, *21*(1). Accessed September 7, 2019 http://csanet.org/newsletter/spring08/nls0803.html.

Engel, S. (2018). April 2018 airstrikes against Syrian chemical-weapons facilities. *Justice.Gov*. https://www.justice.gov/olc/opinion/file/1067551/download.

Evans, J. D.. (1956). Assertion of executive privilege by the Chairman of the Atomic Energy Commission. *Justice Department*. https://www.justice.gov/file/20901/download.

Fahy, C. (1941). Presidential control of wireless and cable information leaving the United States. *Department Of Justice*. https://www.justice.gov/file/20676/download.

Farivar, M. (2020). 3 key takeaways from US Supreme Court rulings on Trump's tax returns. *Voice of America*. https://www.voanews.com/usa/3-key-takeaways-us-supreme-court-rulings-trumps-tax-returns.

Ford, F. (1955). Constitutionality of ajoint resolution requiring the president to propose a balanced budget every year. *Department of Justice*. https://www.justice.gov/file/20736/download.

Forrester, N. A. (2013). *Supplemental Opinions of the office of legal counsel of the United States Department of Justice, Volume 1, 2013*. Washington, DC: Government Printing Office. https://www.justice.gov/olc/file/477221/download.

Fowler, J. (1934). Constitutionality of legislation to confer citizenship upon Albert Einstein. *Justice.Gov*. https://www.justice.gov/file/19176/download.

Freed, K. (1994). Clinton to send troops to Haiti. *Baltimoresun.Com*. https://www.baltimoresun.com/news/bs-xpm-1994-05-11-1994131075-story.html.

Gannon, C. (2017). Temporary certification under the President John F. Kennedy Assassination Records Collection Act of 1992. *Justice.Gov*. https://www.justice.gov/olc/file/1078056/download.

Gannon, C. (2020). Re: Proposed executive order entitled, "Protecting the nation from foreign terrorist entry into the United States." *Politico.Com*. https://www.politico.com/f/?id=0000015a-00dd-deae-a75f-42fd5fd00002.

Garrison, A. (2012). The role of the OLC in providing legal advice to the commander-in-chief after September 11th: The choices made by the Bush administration office of legal counsel. *Journal of the National Association of Administrative Law Judiciary*, *32*(2), 648–718.

Garrison, A. (2013). The opinions by the attorney general and the office of legal counsel: how and why they are significant. *Albany Law Review, 76*(1), 217–245. (Discussed earlier in Proposal)

Garrison, A. (2020). Phone Interview with author. May 27, 2020.

Goldsmith, J. (2009). *The terror presidency: Law and judgement inside the Bush administration*. New York: W.W. Norton and Company.

Hammond, L. (1978). "Presidential appointees—Removal power or disciplinary action—Constitutional Law (Article II, § 2, Cl. 2). *Justice.Gov*. https://www.justice.gov/file/21566/download.

Hammond, L. (1979). Constitutional Law—Constitution—Article V—The Amending Process—The Convention Method. *Justice.Gov*. https://www.justice.gov/file/18351/download.

Harlow *v. Fitzgerald*, 457 U.S. 800 (1982).

Harmon, J. (1977a). Congressional access to tax returns—26 U.S.C. § 6103(F). *Justice.Gov*. https://www.justice.gov/file/21036/download.

Harmon, J. (1977b). Role of the Solicitor General. *Justice.Gov*. https://www.justice.gov/file/21201/download.

Harmon, J. (1978). Freedom of Information Act (5 U.S.C. § 552)—National Security Council—Agency Status under FOIA. *Justice.Gov*. https://www.justice.gov/file/21696/download.

Harmon, J. (1979a). Supplementary discussion of the president's powers relating to the seizure of the American Embassy in Iran. *Justice.Gov*. https://www.justice.gov/file/22316/download.

Harmon, J. (1979b). Constitutional convention—Limitation of power to propose amendments to the constitution. *Justice.Gov*. https://www.justice.gov/file/22181/download.

Harmon, J. (1979c). Presidential powers relating to the situation in Iran. *Justice.Gov*. https://www.justice.gov/file/22311/download.

Harris, S. (2018). The Department of Defense's authority to conduct background investigations for its personnel. *Justice.Gov*. https://www.justice.gov/olc/file/1078041/download.

Harvard Law Review. (2008). Note: The immunity-conferring power of the office of legal counsel. 2008. *Harvard Law Review, 121*(8), 2086–2109.

Jackson, R. (1941). "Wiretapping by members of the Naval Intelligence Service. *Department of Justice*. https://www.justice.gov/file/20886/download.

John F. Kennedy Presidential Library. (2019). Cuban Missile Crisis. *JRK Library*. https://www.jfklibrary.org/learn/about-jfk/jfk-in-history/cuban-missile-crisis.

Johnsen, D. (2004). Functional departmentalism and nonjudicial interpretation: Who determines constitutional meaning?. *Law and Contemporary Problems, 67*(3), 105–148. https://www.repository.law.indiana.edu/cgi/viewcontent.cgi? referer=https://www.google.com/&httpsredir=1&article=1332&context=facpub.

Johnsen, D. (2006). Guidelines for the president's legal advisors (Including "principles to guide the office of legal counsel "). *Indiana Law Journal, 81*(4), 1344–1354.

https://www.repository.law.indiana.edu/cgi/viewcontent.cgi? article=1511&context=ilj.

Judson, H. (1945). Reinstatement of a federal judge following his service in the army. *Justice Department*. https://www.justice.gov/file/20706/download.

Justice.gov. 2011. (2020). *Opinions 2011*. [online] Available at: https://www.justice.gov/olc/opinions?f%5B0%5D=field_opinion_post_date%3A2011 [Accessed 13 May 2020].

Justice.gov. 2012. (2020). *Opinions* 2012 [online] Available at: https://www.justice.gov/olc/opinions?f%5B0%5D=field_opinion_post_date%3A2012 [Accessed 11 May 2020].

Justice.gov. 2014. (2020). *Opinions*. [online] Available at: https://www.justice.gov/olc/opinions?f%5B0%5D=field_opinion_post_date%3A2014 [Accessed 7 May 2020].

Justice.gov. (2020). *Opinions 2010*. [online] Available at: https://www.justice.gov/olc/opinions?f%5B0%5D=field_opinion_post_date%3A2010 [Accessed 12 May 2020].

Katzenbach, N. (1961). Intervention by states and private groups in the internal affairs of another state. *Justice Department*. https://www.justice.gov/file/20771/download.

Katzenbach, N. (1962). Authority of congress to regulate wiretapping by the states. *Justice Department*. https://www.justice.gov/file/20786/download.

Katzenbach, N. (1964). "Use of marshals, troops, and other federal personnel for law enforcement in Mississippi. *Justice Department*. https://www.justicegov/file/20911/download.

Klaidman, D. (2006). Palace revolt. *Newsweek*. https://www.newsweekcom/palace-revolt-113407.

Kleindienst, R. (1970). Supplemental opinions of the office of legal counsel in Volume 1: Effect of a repeal of the Tonkin gulf resolution. *Justice.Gov*. https://www.justice.gov/file/20916/download.

Kmiec, D. (1989). Congressional requests for information from inspectors general concerning open criminal investigations. *Justice.Gov*. https://www.justice.gov/file/24181/download.

Koffsky, D. (2001). Emoluments clause and world bank. *Justice.Gov*. https://www.justice.gov/file/19231/download.

Koffsky, D. (2017). Application of the anti-nepotism statute to a presidential appointment in the White House office. *Justice.Gov*. https://www.justice.gov/olc/file/1085561/download.

Kramer, R. (1961). Authority of the president to blockade Cuba. *Justice Department*. https://www.justice.gov/file/20756/download.

Lawton, M. C. (1974). Presidential or legislative pardon of the president. *Justice.Gov*. https://www.justice.gov/file/20856/download.

Lederman, M. (2009a). *Constitutionality of the Ronald Reagan Centennial Commission Act of 2009*. [online] Justice.gov. Available at: https://www.justice.gov/file/18506/download [Accessed 15 May 2020].

Lederman, M. (2009b). *Constitutionality of the Matthew Shepard hate Crimes Prevention Act.* [online] Justice.gov. Available at: https://www.justice.gov/file/18486/download [Accessed 17 May 2020].

Liptak, A. (2019). "Supreme court says Trump can bar asylum seekers while legal fight continues. *Nytimes.Com.* https://www.nytimes.com/2019/09/11/us/politics/supreme-court-trump-asylum.html.

Luttig, J. M. (1990). Lease or loan of aircraft to foreign countries for assistance in international narcotics control under subsection 506(A)(2) of the Foreign Assistance Act of 1961. *Justice.Gov.* https://www.justice.gov/file/23406/download.

MacLean, A. (1935). Removal of the assistant secretary of commerce by the appointment of a successor. *Department of Justice.* https://www.justice.gov/file/20646/download.

MacLean, A. (1937). Outline of the gold clause cases. *North Carolina Law Review, 15*(3). http://scholarship.law.unc.edu/cgi/viewcontent.cgi? article=1412&context=nclr.

Mittal, S. (2015). OLC's day in court: Judicial deference to the office of legal counsel. *Harvard Law and Policy Review, 9*(1), 211–240.

Morrison, T. (2010). Stare decisis in the office of legal counsel. *Columbia Law Review, 110*(1), 1448–1525. (Former OLC Attorney – Discussed earlier in Proposal)

Morrison, T. (2011). Libya, hostilities, the office of legal counsel, and the process of executive branch legal interpretation. *Harvard Law Review, 124*(7), 62–74.

Olson, T. (1981). Executive power with regard to the Libyan situation. *Justice.Gov.* https://www.justice.gov/file/22861/download.

Opinions of the Office of Legal Counsel of the United States Department of Justice, Vol. 3, 2007. 2014. Washington, DC: Office of Legal Counsel.

Peppard, A. (2015). Tested under fire: How George H.W. Bush asserted control in the wake of the Reagan assassination attempt. *Dallas Morning News.* http://res.dallasnews.com/interactives/reagan-bush/.

Philbin, P. (2001). Legality of the use of military commissions to try terrorists. *Justice.Gov.* https://www.justice.gov/file/19121/download.

Plessy v. Ferguson, 163 US 537, 539 (1896).

Pruitt, S. (2019). How 'duck-and-cover' drills channeled America's cold war anxiety. *History.Com.* https://www.history.com/news/duck-cover-drills-cold-war-arms-race.

Purdy, M. (2015). Who was in control of the government when Ronald Reagan was shot?—Presidential history. *Presidential History.* https://presidentialhistory.com/2015/05/hws-calmness-aftermath-reagan-assassination.html.

Rankin, J. L. (1953). Authority of Florida police officers to make arrests on the basis of FBI pick-up notices. *Justice Department.* https://www.justice.gov/file/20726/download.

Rankin, J. Lee. (1953). Authority of Florida police officers to make arrests on the basis of FBI pick-up notices. *Justice Department.* https://www.justice.gov/file/20731/download.

Rankin, J. L. (1956). Constitutionality of pending bills restricting the withdrawal of public land for national defense. *Department of Justice.* https://www.justice.gov/file/20741/download.

Rehnquist, W. (1970a). Presidential authority to permit incursion into communist sanctuaries in the Cambodia-Vietnam border area. *Justice.Gov.* https://www.justice.gov/file/20821/download.

Rehnquist, W. (1970b). The president and the war power: South Vietnam and the Cambodian sanctuaries. *Justice.Gov.* https://www.justice.gov/file/ 20826/download.

Rhee, J. (2009). *Whether the 10-year minimum sentence in 18 U.S.C. § 924(C)(1)(B)(I) applies to semi-automatic assault weapons.* [online] Justice.gov. Available at: https://www.justice.gov/file/18446/download [Accessed 18 May 2020].

Roosevelt, F. (1933). Outlining the new deal program—May 7, 1933. *Docs.Fdrlibrary.Marist.Edu.* http://docs.fdrlibrary.marist.edu/050733.html.

Saltzman, R. (2010). Executive power and the office of legal counsel. *Yale Law & Policy Review.* https://digitalcommons.law.yale.edu/cgi/viewcontent.cgi?article=1598&context=ylpr.

Schlei, N. (1962). Authority under International Law to take action if the Soviet Union establishes missile bases in Cuba. *Justice Department.* https://www.justice.gov/file/20791/download.

Schuman, D., & Sahar, A. (2018). 39% of Office of Legal Counsel opinions kept from the public. *Medium.* https://medium.com/@danielschuman/39-of-office-of-legal-counsel-opinions-kept-from-the-public-f9c32055e6ab.

Seitz, V. (2013). *Opinions of the Office of Legal Counsel of the United States Department of Justice, Vol 1.* Washington, DC: Office of Legal Counsel.

Simms, L. (1981a). Constitutionality of allowing punishment of misdemeanor by a sentence exceeding one year. *Justice.Gov.* https://www.justice.gov/file/22611/download.

Simms, L. (1981b). https://Www.Justice.Gov/File/22426/Download. *Justice.Gov.* https://www.justice.gov/file/22426/download.

Simms, L. (1981c). Presidential memorandum delaying proposed and pending regulations. *Justice.Gov.* https://www.justice.gov/file/22581/download.

Simms, L. (1981d). Whether the agreement with Iran can be treated as void in part. *Justice.Gov.* https://www.justice.gov/file/22431/download.

Stathis, S. (1982). Presidential disability agreements prior to the 25th amendment. *Presidential Studies Quarterly, 12*(2), 208–215. https://www.jstor.org/stable/27547806?seq=1.

The debates and proceedings and all the laws of a public nature; with a copious index 6Th congress. 1851. Washington, DC: Gales and Seaton.

Thompson, K. (2016). *Application of the recommendations clause to the medicare modernization act.* [online] Justice.gov. Available at: https://www.justice.gov/opinion/file/929881/download [Accessed 9 May 2020].

Townsend, N. (1938). Presidential appearance as a character witness. *Justice Department.* https://www.justice.gov/file/20666/download.

Ulman, L. (1977). Presidential Transition Act (3 USC 102 Note)—Provision of military aircraft and hospital corpsman to a former president (31 USC 638). *Justice.Gov.* https://www.justice.gov/file/21291/download.

Ulman, L. (1981). Restructuring the relationship between the federal government and radio free Europe/radio liberty. *Justice.Gov.* https://www.justice.gov/file/22576/download.

Unknown. (1962). Legal and practical consequences of a blockade of cuba. *Department of Justice.* https://www.justice.gov/file/20906/download.

Varadarajan, S (2019). One year after the SCOTUS ruling: Understanding the muslim ban and how we'll keep fighting it—National Immigration Law Center. *National Immigration Law Center.* https://www.nilc.org/issues/immigration-enforcement/understanding-muslim-ban-one-year-after-ruling/.

Whitaker, H. (2018). Licensing marijuana cultivation in compliance with the single convention on Narcotic Drugs. *Justice.Gov.* https://www.justice.gov/olc/file/1272131/download.

White, W. W. (1957). Applicability of executive privilege to independent regulatory agencies. *Justice Department.* https://www.justice.gov/file/20746/download.

Wilkey, M. (1958). Constitutionality of enrolled bill restricting the withdrawal of public land for national defense. *Justice Department.* https://www.justice.gov/file/20751/download.

Yoo, J. (2001). The president's constitutional authority to conduct military operations against terrorists and nations supporting them. *Justice.Gov.* https://www.justice.gov/file/19151/download.

Recommended Books and Journals

Ackerman, B. (2009). Abolish the White House counsel: And the office of Legal Counsel, too, while we're at it. *Slate Magazine.* https://slate.com/news-and-politics/2009/04/abolish-the-white-house-counsel-and-the-office-of-legal-counsel.html.

Ackerman, B. (2010). *The decline and fall of the American Republic.* Cambridge: Harvard University Press. (Book discusses OLC and calls for reform – leads to written debate between Professors Ackerman and Morrison in Harvard Law Review)

Ackerman, B. (2011). Lost inside the Beltway. *Harvard Law Review, 124*(7), 13–41.

Cover, A. (2012). Supervisory responsibility of the Office of Legal Counsel. Georgetown. *Journal of Legal Ethics, 25*(2), 269–315.

Garrison, A. (2012). The role of the OLC in providing legal advice to the commander-in-chief after September 11th: The choices made by the Bush Administration Office of Legal Counsel. *Journal of the National Association of Administrative Law Judiciary, 32*(2), 648–718.

Garrison, A. (2013). The opinions by the Attorney General and the Office of Legal Counsel: How and why they are significant. *Albany Law Review, 76*(1), 217–245. (Discussed earlier in Proposal)

Goitein, Elizabeth and the Brennan Center for Justice. (2016). The new era of secret law. Accessed March 15, 2018. https://www.brennancenter.org/sites/default/files/publications/The_New_Era_of_Secret_Law.pdf.

Goldsmith, J. (2009). *The terror presidency: Law and judgement inside the Bush administration*. New York: W.W. Norton and Company.

Goldsmith, J. (2012). *Power and constraint: The accountable presidency after 9/11*. New York: W.W. Norton and Company.

Lavitt, J. (2010). The crime of conviction of John Choon Yoo: The actual criminality in the OLC during the Bush administration. *Maine Law Review, 62*(1), 155–198.

Mittal, S. (2015). OLC's day in court: Judicial deference to the Office of Legal Counsel. *Harvard Law and Policy Review, 9*(1), 211–240.

Morrison, T. (2011). Constitutional alarmism. *Harvard Law Review, 124*(7), 1688–1749. (Book Review of Ackerman book listed above)

Yoo, J. (2007). *War by other means*. New York: Grove/Atlantic, Inc.

Yoo, J. (2008). *The powers of war and peace: The constitution and foreign affairs after 9/11*. Chicago, IL: University of Chicago Press.

STUDIES IN LAW AND POLITICS

The Studies in Law and Politics series is devoted to texts and monographs that explore the multidimensional and multidisciplinary areas of law and politics. Subject matters to be addressed in this series include, but will not be limited to: constitutional law; civil rights and liberties issues; law, race, gender, and gender orientation studies; law and ethics; women and the law; judicial behavior and decision-making; legal theory; sociology of law; comparative legal systems; criminal justice; courts and the political process; and other topics on the law and the political process that would be of interest to law and politics scholars. Submission of single-author and collaborative studies, as well as collections of essays are invited.

For additional information about this series or for the submission of manuscripts, please contact:

Peter Lang Publishing, Inc.
Acquisitions Department
editorial@peterlang.com

To order other books in this series, please contact our Customer Service Department:

peterlang@presswarehouse.com (within the U.S.)
orders@peterlang.com (outside the U.S.)

Or browse online by series:

www.peterlang.com

www.ingramcontent.com/pod-product-compliance
Ingram Content Group UK Ltd.
Pitfield, Milton Keynes, MK11 3LW, UK
UKHW021827100926
8556IPUK00003B/210

9 781433 184888